MindPlan

Mental Health Matters

A catalogue record of this book is available from the British Library.

ISBN: 979-8-87591-817-9

ABOUT THE AUTHOR: ANGELO SOTERIOU
A Passionate Advocate for Mental Wellness

My name is Angelo Soteriou, and my journey in mental health is both personal and professional. As a survivor who has battled and overcome depression and anxiety, I stand as a testament to the power of the techniques detailed in this book. My experiences have not only shaped my understanding of mental health but have also fuelled my dedication to helping others navigate similar challenges. As a professional Solution-Focused Clinical Hypnotherapist and Psychotherapist, I specialise in the mental health sector, dedicating my career to helping individuals navigate and overcome their mental health challenges.

Educational and Professional Background

My journey in the field of hypnotherapy and psychotherapy began at The Clifton Practice, a renowned UK and international training body. Here, I received my Hypnotherapy in Practice Diploma (HPD), a program acclaimed for its rigorous and practical approach. The diploma is accredited by the Northern Council for Further Education (NCFE), ensuring the highest standards in hypnotherapy education.

I have garnered extensive knowledge and experience in this field. Alongside my HPD, I have earned a Diploma in Solution-Focused Hypnotherapy (DSFH) and a General Qualification in Hypnotherapy Practice (GQHP).

Professional Affiliations and Accreditations

My commitment to professional excellence is reflected in my memberships and registrations with several esteemed organisations:

- Association for Solution-Focused Hypnotherapy (AfSFH)
- Institute of Health Management (MIHM)

- Complementary and Natural Healthcare Council (CNHC), approved by the Professional Standards Authority for Health and Social Care
- National Council for Hypnotherapy (MNCH)
- General Hypnotherapy Standards Council (GHSC)
- General Hypnotherapy Register (GHR)

These affiliations not only speak to my dedication to the field but also ensure adherence to the highest standards of practice and ethics.

Specialisation in Solution-Focused Hypnotherapy

Solution-Focused Hypnotherapy, a blend of psychotherapy and hypnosis, is the cornerstone of my Practice. This approach, grounded in the latest research in neuroscience and incorporating elements of Solution-Focused Techniques, Brain Based Therapy, Cognitive Behavioural Therapy (CBT), and Neuro-Linguistic Programming (NLP), offers a holistic path to mental wellness.

A Personal Mission

My choice to specialise in mental health stems from a deep understanding of the impact mental health disorders have on everyday life. I am passionate about making a difference and believe that Solution-Focused Hypnotherapy is a profoundly effective way to transform lives. Changing lives for the better is not just my profession; it's my calling and the most rewarding endeavour I can imagine.

Commitment to Professional Integrity

As a practitioner, I uphold the highest standards of integrity and professionalism.

In this book, I bring together my expertise and passion, offering readers a compassionate guide to navigating and overcoming mental health challenges with the power of Solution-Focused Therapy.

ACKNOWLEDGEMENTS

I am profoundly grateful for the support and inspiration I received while writing *MINDPLAN*. First, I extend my deepest thanks to my family and friends for their unwavering support and belief in my vision. Their encouragement was a beacon during the challenging moments of this journey.

Special appreciation goes to my peers and mentors in the field of Solution-Focused Clinical Hypnotherapy and Psychotherapy. Their insights and wisdom have been invaluable in shaping the concepts and practices outlined in this book.

Some references draws heavily from training, materials & course notes in the area of Solution-Focused Hypnotherapy produced by The Clifton Practice in Bristol. Credit is due to David Newton, whose insights as well as my professional experience form the basis of this book.

David Newton is the founder of The Clifton Practice where I studied and achieved my Solution-Focused Hypnotherapy Practitioners Diploma.

I extend my sincere gratitude to Giorgio Trovato for the use of his image on the cover of my book. His talents and generosity are deeply appreciated.

I must also acknowledge the countless individuals who bravely shared their stories of mental health struggles and triumphs.

Lastly, I extend my gratitude to you, the reader. Your decision to embark on this journey of understanding and self-improvement is a step towards a brighter future. May *MINDPLAN* be a valuable companion on your path to mental wellness.

CONTENTS

INTRODUCTION TO MINDPLAN
Welcome to Your Journey of Healing and Growth

Dear Esteemed Reader,

Let us embark on an incredible journey of self-discovery and healing with *MINDPLAN*, your personal haven of wisdom and guidance. This book isn't just a mere collection of pages; it's a compassionate companion on your journey, a wise mentor whispering insights, and a roadmap leading you towards a life filled with harmony and joy.

As you turn the pages of *MINDPLAN*, you'll discover a wealth of knowledge and heartfelt advice. Each section is like a stepping stone on your path to a more peaceful and fulfilling life. Whether you're looking for ways to calm your mind, strategies to overcome anxiety, or insights to understand your emotions better, *MINDPLAN* is here to assist you. It's a guide that listens, understands, and helps you navigate the complexities of your inner world.

Why the Name *MINDPLAN*?

The answer lies in the very heart of what this book represents. *MINDPLAN* is more than just a title; it encapsulates a philosophy, a way of approaching life's mental challenges with a proactive and solution-oriented mind-set.

Imagine *MINDPLAN* as a master architect of mental wellness. Just as an architect meticulously drafts a blueprint to construct a solid, functional, and beautiful building, *MINDPLAN* offers you a carefully structured framework. This framework is designed to help you build and fortify your mental resilience, stone by stone, thought by thought. It's about laying a strong foundation for your mental health, then adding the walls and roof of coping strategies, understanding, and self-care.

The answer lies in the very heart of what this book represents. *MINDPLAN* is more than just a title; it encapsulates a philosophy, a way of approaching life's mental challenges with a proactive and solution-oriented mind-set.

Imagine *MINDPLAN* as a master architect of mental wellness. Just as an architect meticulously drafts a blueprint to construct a solid, functional, and beautiful building, *MINDPLAN* offers you a carefully structured framework. This framework is designed to help you build and fortify your mental resilience, brick by brick, thought by thought. It's about laying a strong foundation for your mental health, then adding the walls and roof of coping strategies, understanding, and self-care.

The Beginning of Your *MINDPLAN* Journey

As we stand at the threshold of a transformative chapter in your life, let us initiate this remarkable journey together, a journey teeming with hope and determination. Your *MINDPLAN* odyssey commences at this very moment, a significant step towards a future filled with self-discovery, personal growth, and inner peace.

As your guide, I pledge to be there for you every step of the way. In moments of uncertainty, *MINDPLAN* will offer you support; in times of triumph, it will share your joy. We will explore the depths of your inner world, uncovering strengths and potentials perhaps yet unknown to you.

Together, we will empower you to face life's challenges with confidence and grace.

With heartfelt warmth and unwavering encouragement,

Angelo Soteriou

"In the midst of depression, anxiety, and stress, remember that you are not alone. Your strength is in recognising the storm but also in knowing that beneath it, calm waters await. It's not about silencing the storm, but about learning to dance in the rain."

- Angelo Soteriou

Chapter 1: The Roots of Depression
Overview of Depression

Depression: More Than Just Sadness

When we hear the word "depression," many of us think of deep sadness or a blue mood. But it's so much more than that. Depression is like a shadow that dims life's colours and drains energy, hope, and motivation. It's not just a bad day; it's a persistent cloud that affects how we feel, think, and handle daily activities.

A Common Misunderstanding

There's a common misunderstanding that depression is simply about feeling sad and that one should be able to snap out of it with enough willpower. But it's not a sign of weakness or a character flaw. Just like a cold or the flu, depression is a genuine health condition, and it can affect anyone, regardless of age, gender, or background.

One crucial distinction is between feeling depressed and suffering from clinical depression. It's common to say "I'm feeling depressed" after a rough day or a disappointing event. These feelings are valid and part of the human experience, but they are typically short-lived, shifting as circumstances change.

In contrast, clinical depression is a persistent psychological condition. It's like being stuck in a dense fog that doesn't lift with time or even with positive life changes. This distinction is vital because it shapes how we approach healing and growth. Recognising the difference empowers us to seek appropriate support and strategies for each.

How It Feels

Imagine waking up every day feeling like you're under a heavy blanket, where even the smallest tasks feel overwhelming. Joy and laughter may seem like memories from another life. People experiencing depression often describe it as living in a fog or having a constant sense of impending doom. It can make the world seem colourless and life feel pointless.

It's Not a One-Size-Fits-All

Depression doesn't look the same for everyone. For some, it's a lingering low mood, a sense of perpetual fatigue, or a loss of interest in things once loved. For others, it manifests as irritability, sleep disturbances, or a change in appetite. It's this variability that sometimes makes depression hard to recognise, both for the people experiencing it and their loved ones.

The Good News

Here's the uplifting part: depression is treatable. Just as a plant withers without sunlight but revives with care and sunshine, people with depression can regain their colour and vitality with the right support and treatment. In the upcoming chapters, we'll explore how to step out of the shadow of depression and embrace life's vibrancy again.

Key Factors Contributing to Depression

1. Personal Life: When Life Throws a Curveball

Life is unpredictable, and sometimes it throws curveballs that can knock us off our feet. Major life events, both negative and positive, can trigger depression. This could be the loss of a loved one, a difficult breakup, or even significant changes like moving to a new city or starting a new job. These events can evoke strong emotions and stress, sometimes leading to depression, especially if they cause a significant shift in our daily lives or self-identity.

2. Biological Aspects: It's Not Just 'In Your Head'

Depression often has roots that go deeper than our immediate circumstances. Our biology plays a crucial role. For instance, genetics can make some people more prone to depression – it can run in families, much like the colour of our eyes or our height. Then there's brain chemistry, the complex dance of chemicals in our brains. When these chemicals are out of balance, it can affect our mood, thoughts, and emotions. It's important to remember that these biological factors are not something we can just 'wish away' any more than we could change our height or eye colour.

3. Lifestyle and Environment: The World Around Us

Our daily environment and lifestyle choices also weigh heavily on our mental health. A stressful job, long hours, or an unhealthy work-life balance can be significant contributors. Social factors like isolation, lack of support, or challenging family dynamics play a role too. Even habitual patterns like poor sleep, a sedentary lifestyle, or an unhealthy diet can subtly but significantly impact our mood and mental well-being over time.

Examples: Everyday Scenarios Leading to Depression

1. The Overwhelmed Parent

Imagine Jill, a single parent juggling a full-time job and raising two young children. Recently, she's been feeling constantly exhausted, struggling to keep up with her responsibilities. The demands of her job, coupled with sleepless nights and financial worries, have left her feeling hopeless and drained. Jill's situation exemplifies how chronic stress and overwhelming responsibilities can lead to symptoms of depression.

2. The Recent Graduate Facing Uncertainty

Meet Alex, who recently graduated from college. While this should be an exciting new chapter, Alex feels lost and unsure about the future. Most of his friends have moved away, and job rejections have started to weigh heavily on his self-esteem. This sense of uncertainty and isolation is a common trigger for depression in young adults, as they navigate major life transitions.

3. The Corporate Executive with High Stress

John is a high-level executive in a bustling corporation. On the surface, he has it all - a successful career, a beautiful home, and a loving family. However, the constant pressure and long hours at work have started to take a toll. He's irritable, has lost interest in hobbies, and feels disconnected from his family. John's case highlights how even those who seem to have everything can struggle with depression, often driven by high stress and a lack of work-life balance.

4. The Widow Coping with Loss

Linda, a retired teacher, recently lost her husband of 40 years to a long illness. Since his passing, she finds herself struggling with deep sadness and a lack of motivation to engage in activities they used to enjoy together. Her story is a poignant example of how significant life events, like the loss of a loved one, can lead to depression, particularly in older adults.

A Message of Hope and Resilience

There's Light Beyond the Fog

As we reach the end of this section, it's essential to remember that while the journey through depression can be challenging, it is also one of hope and potential for change. The stories and scenarios we've shared might resonate with your experiences, reflecting the complexities and struggles that come with depression. But within these stories also lies the message that improvement and management are not just possibilities but realities for many.

The Power of Small Steps

Overcoming depression often begins with small, yet significant steps. It's about finding that one thing each day that brings a sense of accomplishment or joy, no matter how small. Whether it's going for a walk, reconnecting with an old friend, or simply taking a moment for yourself, these small steps can start to turn the tide against depression.

Embracing Support and Strategies

Remember, you don't have to walk this path alone. There's immense strength in seeking support, be it from loved ones, support groups, or mental health professionals. Coupled with effective strategies and treatments, ranging from therapy and medication to lifestyle changes and self-care practices, there's a whole arsenal available to combat depression.

A Journey Towards Healing

Depression is not a life sentence. It's a condition that you can manage and overcome with time, effort, and the right approach. As you continue reading *MINDPLAN*, you'll discover various tools and techniques to guide you on this journey. With each page, we aim to empower you with knowledge, strategies, and most importantly, the belief that a brighter, more joyful life is within reach.

You Are Stronger Than You Think

You possess an inner resilience that's stronger than you might realise. With each step forward, you're moving towards a place of better mental health and well-being. We're here to support you on this journey, to celebrate your victories, and to remind you that there's always hope and a path forward.

Chapter 2: Understanding Anxiety

What is Anxiety? Separating It from Normal Stress

As we turn the page to a new chapter, let us shift our focus to a common but often misunderstood condition: anxiety. Understanding anxiety is crucial because it affects how we approach and manage it in our lives.

Anxiety: More Than Just Worry

At some point, everyone feels worried or stressed. Maybe it's before a big presentation, during a financial crunch, or when facing a challenging situation. This kind of stress is a normal reaction to external pressures and typically fades away once the situation is resolved.

Anxiety, however, is different. It's like an alarm system that's too sensitive, going off frequently and often without a clear reason. It's a persistent sense of unease or fear that interferes with daily life. Unlike normal stress, anxiety doesn't always dissipate when the external situation improves or changes. It lingers, creating a chronic sense of dread or apprehension about things that may seem trivial to others.

The Persistent Echo of Anxiety

Imagine a scenario where you're constantly on edge, worrying about things that might never happen. You might feel your heart racing, experience shortness of breath, or have trouble concentrating, even in the absence of any immediate threat or pressure. This is the world of someone living with anxiety: a place where the mind is often caught in a loop of worry and fear, making everyday life feel more challenging.

Anxiety's Many Faces

It's also important to recognise that anxiety isn't a one-size-fits-all condition. It manifests in various forms, from generalised anxiety disorder, where the worry is broad and pervasive, to specific phobias or panic disorders, where the anxiety is triggered by specific situations or objects. Understanding these nuances is key to demystifying the experience of anxiety and finding effective ways to manage it.

Common Causes: Triggers of Anxiety

Navigating the Triggers of Anxiety

Anxiety, like a shadow, can follow us through various stages and situations in life. Understanding its common triggers is crucial, as it helps us identify and address the root causes. Let's explore some of these typical triggers in a way that's relatable and easy to understand.

1. Life Changes: The Winds of Change

Change, even when positive, can be a significant trigger for anxiety. Moving to a new city, starting a new job, or entering a new phase of life like parenthood or retirement are all monumental changes that can stir up anxiety. It's the uncertainty and the need to adapt to new circumstances that can leave us feeling unsettled and anxious.

Example: Consider Maya, who just started college. Away from home for the first time, she's facing new responsibilities, a different environment, and the challenge of making new friends. These changes, while exciting, also bring a level of anxiety about fitting in and managing her new life.

2. Work Stress: The Daily Grind

The workplace is a common source of stress and anxiety for many. Tight deadlines, heavy workloads, challenging relationships with colleagues or supervisors, and fear of job instability can contribute to a constant state of worry and tension.

Example: Think of Tom, a graphic designer with tight deadlines. The pressure to deliver perfect work, combined with long hours and a demanding boss, keeps his mind in a perpetual state of anxiety, affecting his sleep and personal life.

3. Personal Challenges: Life's Hurdles

Personal challenges, whether they're financial difficulties, health concerns, or relationship issues, can also be significant triggers. These situations often feel overwhelming and out of our control, fuelling anxiety.

Example: Emily is dealing with financial strain after a recent job loss. The uncertainty of how to pay bills and support her family is a constant source of anxiety, making it hard for her to focus on finding new employment.

4. Social Situations: The Social Spotlight

For some, social interactions, from attending parties to public speaking, can trigger anxiety. This is often rooted in a fear of judgment or not living up to others' expectations.

Example: Terry, who is generally shy, finds social gatherings nerve-wracking. The thought of being in a crowd or having to make small talk triggers his anxiety, leading him to avoid social events.

Anxiety in Everyday Life

The Subtle Ways Anxiety Creeps In

Anxiety isn't always about big, overwhelming fears. Often, it's the smaller, everyday situations where anxiety can creep in subtly, yet persistently. Let's explore some relatable examples to understand how anxiety can manifest in day-to-day life.

1. The Morning Routine: Starting the Day on an Anxious Note

Imagine Lisa, who starts each day with a sense of dread. As soon as her alarm goes off, her mind races with thoughts about all she has to accomplish. Even routine tasks like making breakfast or getting dressed can feel overwhelming. Her morning anxiety sets a challenging tone for the rest of her day, impacting her focus and mood.

2. The Supermarket: A Common Setting for Anxiety

Supermarket shopping seems simple, but for Jack, it's a different story. He becomes anxious about making the right choices, navigating crowds, or interacting with cashiers. The aisles feel like a maze, and the hustle and bustle of shoppers intensifies his anxiety, turning a routine errand into a stressful ordeal.

3. Social Media: A Modern Source of Anxiety

Social media is a part of daily life for many, including Emma. She often finds herself scrolling through feeds, comparing her life to others'. This comparison leads to feelings of inadequacy and anxiety, making her question her own accomplishments and worth.

4. Evening Wind-Down: Anxiety Instead of Relaxation

Evenings are meant for relaxation, but for Aiden, they bring a different experience. As he tries to unwind, his mind gets flooded with worries about the next day, uncompleted tasks, or unresolved issues. Instead of resting, he spends hours tossing and turning, plagued by anxious thoughts.

5. The Unexpected Call: Triggering Anxiety

When Zoe sees an unexpected call from her family, her heart immediately races with worry. Even though it's often nothing serious, the mere unpredictability of these calls triggers her anxiety, leaving her apprehensive every time her phone rings.

Hopeful Message: Embracing Hope in Managing Anxiety

A Light in the Maze of Anxiety

As we wrap up this chapter on understanding anxiety, it's important to remember that while anxiety can be a complex and challenging part of life, it is also highly manageable. There is always a path forward, a light in what can sometimes feel like a maze of worries and fears.

Anxiety is Not Your Destiny

First and foremost, know that anxiety does not define you. It's a part of your journey, but it's not the entirety of your story. Countless individuals have walked this path before you and have found ways to manage and thrive despite their anxiety. You are capable of doing the same.

Small Steps Lead to Big Changes

Managing anxiety often starts with small, yet powerful steps. It could be as simple as recognising when your thoughts are spiralling into worry and taking a moment to pause and breathe. Gradually, you'll learn techniques to calm your mind, challenge anxious thoughts, and face situations that once seemed daunting.

Embrace Support and Understanding

Remember, seeking help is a sign of strength, not weakness. Whether it's talking to a trusted friend, joining a support group, or consulting with a mental health professional, getting support can be a game-changer in managing anxiety. You're not meant to navigate this alone.

A Journey of Growth

Every step you take in understanding and managing your anxiety is a step towards growth. With each day, you're gaining more tools and insights to help you cope better. You're learning resilience, empathy, and self-awareness – qualities that will not only help you in dealing with anxiety but also enrich your life in countless other ways.

Hold Onto Hope

So, hold onto hope. The journey might have its ups and downs, but with each step, you're moving towards a life where anxiety doesn't hold the reins. You're moving towards a future where you're in control, empowered, and free to live your life with joy and purpose.

Chapter 3: Stress and Its Triggers
Defining Stress: Understanding Its Role in Our Lives

Stress: A Common Experience

As we delve into the topic of stress, it's important to recognise it as a universal experience. Stress is a natural response of our body and mind to demands or challenges. It's not inherently negative – in fact, stress can be a motivating force, helping us respond to threats, meet deadlines, or push through difficult situations.

The Two Faces of Stress

Stress can be categorised into two types: eustress and distress. Eustress, or positive stress, occurs when our response to a challenge is motivating and energising. It's the kind of stress you feel when you're excited or engaged in a productive activity. On the other hand, distress, or negative stress, happens when challenges overwhelm our ability to cope. This is the stress that feels draining and can lead to feelings of anxiety, frustration, or despair.

How Stress Works

When faced with a stressor, our body reacts in a specific way. This reaction, often called the 'fight or flight' response, involves a series of physiological changes like increased heart rate and heightened senses. These changes are designed to help us respond to immediate challenges. In small doses, this response is beneficial. However, problems arise when this response is constantly triggered by the ongoing challenges of modern life.

The Role of Stress in Modern Life

In today's fast-paced world, stress is a common part of life. It can stem from various sources – work pressures, financial concerns, relationship issues, or even daily commutes. While a certain level of stress is normal and even necessary, excessive or chronic stress can take a toll on our physical and mental health.

Everyday Stressors: The Common Sources of Stress

Navigating the Stress of Daily Life

In our journey to understand stress, recognising the common sources that many of us encounter is crucial. These everyday stressors, while part of normal life, can accumulate and impact our mental and physical well-being if not managed effectively.

1. Job Pressure: The Workplace Challenge

For many, the workplace is a significant source of stress. Deadlines, performance expectations, office politics, and the constant need to juggle multiple tasks can create a high-stress environment. Even those who love their jobs can experience work-related stress, affecting their productivity and overall job satisfaction.

Example: Leo, a project manager, often finds himself overwhelmed by tight deadlines and the pressure to meet client expectations. His job, while rewarding, often leads to long hours and work-related stress that spills over into his personal life.

2. Family Dynamics: Navigating Relationships

Family life, though a source of joy and support, can also be a source of stress. Balancing the needs of different family members, dealing with conflicts, or managing the demands of parenting and caregiving can create a stressful home environment.

Example: Anita, a mother of two, constantly finds herself trying to balance her children's activities, her marriage, and her aging parents' health needs. The constant need to be there for everyone puts a strain on her, leading to stress.

3. Financial Concerns: The Weight of Money Matters

Financial issues are a common stressor for many people. Concerns about paying bills, saving for the future, or dealing with debt can lead to constant worry and anxiety about financial stability.

Example: Carlos, recently laid off, is stressed about making ends meet and supporting his family. The uncertainty of his financial future weighs heavily on his mind, affecting his sleep and daily mood.

4. Health Worries: When Well-being Causes Worry

Personal health or the health of loved ones can be a significant source of stress. Chronic illnesses, unexpected health issues, or caring for someone with a health condition can create ongoing worry and stress.

Example: Ellie, diagnosed with a chronic illness, often feels stressed about managing her condition and the impact it has on her lifestyle and future plans.

Stress in the Modern World

The Fast-Paced Nature of Today's Life

In this era of technological advancements and rapid change, modern life brings with it unique challenges and stressors. Understanding how our contemporary lifestyle contributes to stress is key to managing it effectively.

The Digital Connection: A Double-Edged Sword

Technology has connected us in unprecedented ways, but it also brings a new kind of stress. The constant barrage of emails, social media notifications, and the pressure to be always 'on' can lead to digital overload. This constant connectivity can make it difficult to disconnect, relax, and recharge, increasing our stress levels.

Example: Karen, a marketing executive, finds herself constantly checking her phone for work emails, even during off-hours. The inability to unplug makes her feel like she's always at work, blurring the boundaries between her professional and personal life.

The Information Overload: Navigating a Sea of Data

The sheer amount of information available at our fingertips is overwhelming. While being informed is beneficial, the endless stream of news, especially negative news, can be a constant source of stress, contributing to feelings of anxiety and worry about the world.

Example: Anthony finds himself habitually scrolling through news feeds, absorbing a barrage of distressing news stories. This habit leaves him feeling increasingly anxious about global issues, impacting his mood and outlook on life.

The Pace of Change: Keeping Up with a Rapidly Evolving World

The rapid pace of change in today's world can be disorienting and stressful. From keeping up with the latest technology to adapting to changing social norms and work demands, the pressure to stay current and adaptable can be a significant source of stress.

Example: Laura, in her mid-fifties, struggles to keep up with the changing technologies at her workplace. She feels a constant pressure to adapt, fearing that she might fall behind her younger colleagues.

The Quest for Balance: Juggling Multiple Roles

Modern life often requires juggling multiple roles and responsibilities. Balancing work, family, personal health, and social obligations can be a challenging act, leading to a feeling of being stretched too thin.

Example: John, a father of three, finds himself torn between his demanding job, supporting his partner, and being present for his children. The struggle to maintain balance often leaves him feeling stressed and exhausted.

Positive Spin: Recognising Stress and Looking Ahead

Understanding the Signals of Stress

As we wrap up our exploration of stress in modern life, it's crucial to recognise its signs and signals in our own lives. Stress can manifest in various ways: it might be physical symptoms like headaches or fatigue, emotional signs like irritability or mood swings, or behavioural changes such as withdrawing from social activities or changes in eating habits. Becoming aware of these signs is the first step in taking control.

Tips for Spotting Stress

1. **Listen to Your Body:** Often, our bodies will signal stress before our minds fully acknowledge it. Pay attention to physical signs like muscle tension, headaches, or sleep disturbances.
2. **Monitor Your Thoughts**: Notice if your thoughts are constantly negative, worried, or anxious. This mental pattern can be a clear indicator of stress.
3. **Observe Your Behaviours:** Changes in your behaviour, like snapping at loved ones, neglecting hobbies, or relying on substances like alcohol, can be signs of underlying stress.

A Sneak Peek into Managing Stress

Now that we've identified the sources and signs of stress, what's next? How do we navigate this landscape of modern stressors without losing our sense of peace and joy? The upcoming chapters of *MINDPLAN* are dedicated to answering these questions.

What to Look Forward To

Strategies for Stress Management: Learn practical and effective strategies to manage and reduce stress in your life.

Building Resilience: Discover how to build resilience, allowing you to bounce back more effectively from stressful situations.

Creating a Balanced Life: Find out how to create a more balanced lifestyle that supports your mental and physical well-being.

Empowerment is Within Reach

Remember, while stress is an inevitable part of life, being overwhelmed by it is not. You have the power to change how you respond to stress. The upcoming chapters will equip you with the tools and knowledge to transform your relationship with stress, opening the door to a more balanced and fulfilling life.

Stay tuned for empowering insights and practical tips that will guide you toward a journey of balance and resilience.

Chapter 4: What Causes Stress, Anxiety & Depression?

To answer this question, we must first understand how the brain works.

What many people don't know is that, although we have one brain, for all intents and purposes we actually have two minds – The Intellectual Mind and the Primitive Mind.

THE INTELLECTUAL MIND

Welcome to an exploration of your Intellectual Mind, the very essence of your conscious self. This part of you is not just an observer but an active participant in the world, linked to an immense reservoir of intellectual capacity.

The emergence of our Intellectual Mind, whether through a twist of genetic fate or the march of evolution, marked a pivotal moment in human history. It bestowed upon us the gift of imagination and foresight. Imagine the ability to not just exist, but to dream, to envision a future shaped by our actions. This was a game-changer, setting us apart from our evolutionary cousins and propelling humanity forward at an unprecedented pace.

Our predecessors learned by instinct, but we have evolved to learn through experience and imagination. This ability to mentally simulate outcomes, to learn not just from what has happened but from what could happen, has been a driving force in our progress. It's what makes us inventors, dreamers, creators. Each step we took as effective hunter-gatherers, each successful strategy we devised, contributed not just to our survival but to the flourishing of our species as a whole.

When you engage with life through your Intellectual Mind, you're tapping into a source of great wisdom and positivity. This is where you weigh situations thoughtfully, find solutions, and make decisions that align with your best self. It's the part of you that looks at a challenge and sees an opportunity for growth and learning.

THE PRIMITIVE BRAIN & THE LIMBIC SYSTEM

In the realm of self-discovery and personal growth, it's essential to understand the dual nature of our brain – the intellectual and the primitive. While we have evolved intellectually, our primitive brain, deeply rooted in instinct, continues to play a significant role in our lives.

Think of early humans, for whom survival hinged on vigilance and physical strength. Today, our intellectual advancements have led us to face more complex dangers. But with this progress, our limbic system, the seat of our instinctual responses, remains highly reactive, not just to real threats but also to our thoughts and imagination.

At the heart of our primitive brain lies the amygdala, the command centre for our instinctual reactions, often referred to as the fight, flight, or freeze responses. This primal area works closely with the hippocampus, which stores our instinctual behaviours and patterns, and the hypothalamus, which regulates the body's chemical responses.

Picture this scenario: you step outside and suddenly encounter a lion. Your body reacts instinctively – heart racing, sweating, stomach churning – as you prepare to flee. This reaction, while extreme, is entirely appropriate for such a dangerous situation.

However, this same response mechanism activates in everyday life when we face heightened anxiety. The primitive brain takes the reins, often leading us to react with fear, anxiety, depression, or anger. It's a direct link between our anxiety levels and our ability to maintain intellectual control. When faced with extreme danger, the alarm system in our brain shifts control from the pre-frontal cortex, the centre of intellectual reasoning, to the limbic system, our primitive response centre.

Our primitive mind steps in during perceived crises or emergencies, often as a protective measure. But these responses – depression, anxiety, and anger – can sometimes be misaligned with the actual situation at hand.

PATTERN MATCHING

In the fascinating journey of self-help and personal growth, understanding the concept of 'pattern matching' is a game changer. It's a process ingrained in both the intellectual and primitive parts of our brain, playing a crucial role in how we perceive and interact with the world.

Imagine your brain as a master organiser, constantly sifting through experiences, trying to make sense of them. It does this through pattern matching, where it aligns new experiences with existing templates or patterns – some of which we're born with. The intellectual side of our brain strives for growth and improvement, continually updating these templates for our betterment.

On the flip side, our limbic system, which includes the amygdala and hippocampus, is like a vigilant sentinel. It's always scanning our environment, comparing incoming sensory information against survival templates or fear memories. Is a situation life-threatening or life-enhancing? This system decides. For instance, a simple rustle in the bushes could trigger an alarm response, thanks to a past experience where a similar sound signalled danger.

Our experiences, especially emotional ones, get processed and stored in the hippocampus. When we encounter deeply traumatic events, the intense emotional reaction imprints these memories in our limbic system, tagging them as potentially life-threatening. This leads to the creation of a 'template' in our brain to avoid such events in the future. When a current experience even partially matches this template, our amygdala activates an alarm response, often at a subconscious level. This is how deep-seated fears and phobias can take root.

HOW WE DO OUR THINKING

Let's delve into the fascinating realm of how we think and process events in our lives. Contrary to what one might assume, it's not always the events themselves that spark a sense of crisis within us. This becomes evident when we consider that not everyone responds to the same situation, like the challenges of university life, with anxiety or panic. This leads us to a profound realisation: it's the patterns of our thoughts surrounding these events that shape our emotional responses.

Let's travel back in time to our cave-dwelling ancestors. Faced with harsh weather conditions or lurking dangers outside the cave, they had a simple but effective response – they stayed put, under the safety of their shelters, waiting for the situation to change. This basic instinctive reaction has evolved over time into the complex emotions we experience today, such as depression, phobia, fear, and anxiety.

Imagine if we were still living in a jungle-like environment, constantly on edge. Our response system would be akin to having a 'panic button' always within reach. Anger, in this context, can be seen as an archaic tool – a surge of strength to defend ourselves against predators or threats from rival groups.

MODEL OF THE WORLD (MAP) - OUR SUBJECTIVE VIEW

Our perception of the world, often shaped more by our internal maps than by the world itself. This idea is well encapsulated in a popular phrase from Neuro-Linguistic Programming (NLP): "The map is not the territory."

This concept suggests that there's often a mismatch between reality and how we perceive it. For instance, an overly optimistic attitude might not serve us well in a dangerous situation, like encountering a lion. Conversely, excessive pessimism can spiral into fear, anxiety, and unhappiness. Our individual worldview, or 'map', is shaped by various factors and constraints as highlighted by Dr. Richard Bandler:

[23]

- **Neurological Constraints**: Our sensory inputs – sight, sound, touch, smell, and taste – provide us with information about the world. Yet, each of us tends to favour one or two of these senses over the others, influencing our perception of reality.
- **Social Constraints**: The language we grow up with shapes our understanding of the world. The more nuanced our language, the more detailed and rich our experiences become.
- **Individual Constraints**: Our unique life experiences shape our likes, dislikes, habits, beliefs, and values. Each person's journey is different, leading to a distinctive view of the world.

Our perception is also influenced by three critical filters: deletion, distortion, and generalisation. These processes help us manage the influx of information so we're not overwhelmed. However, problems arise when these filters eliminate, alter, or oversimplify the wrong pieces of information, leading to perceptions that can either hinder or harm our well-being.

It's crucial to note that our communication consists of only 7% words, with 38% tone and 55% body language. This composition further shapes our interpretation of the world and interactions with others.

PRIMITIVE MIND = NEGATIVE MIND

This part of our brain is hardwired to perceive the world through a lens of caution and scepticism, an evolutionary trait designed to ensure our survival.

Think of the primitive mind as your internal alarm system, always on the lookout for potential threats. For instance, in the face of a real danger like encountering a lion, this part of your brain jumps into action with a clear message: "Danger ahead! Protect yourself!" This instinctual response is invaluable in genuinely perilous situations, but it becomes problematic when applied to everyday scenarios.

When confronted with modern-day stressors like financial worries, job uncertainties, or interpersonal conflicts, the primitive mind often overreacts. It sees these challenges not as manageable situations, but as dire threats, triggering a cascade of negative emotions and reactions. This mind-set can turn into a constant loop of worry and stress, keeping you in a state of perpetual alert.

Moreover, the primitive mind tends to be repetitive and obsessive. If it perceives a threat, it fixates on it, leading to constant worry and vigilance. This aspect of our mind lacks innovation and creativity; it prefers to stick to known patterns and behaviours that ensured our survival in the past. This can result in a reluctance to embrace change or try new approaches, even when the old ways are no longer effective or relevant.

HOW DO WE CREATE THIS ANXIETY?

Understanding the intricate relationship between our thoughts and anxiety is paramount. At the heart of this relationship is a profound yet often overlooked truth: our mind's inability to differentiate between what is real and what is imagined. This aspect of human psychology is not just a curious trait; it's a crucial element in shaping our perceptions, emotions, and, ultimately, our reality.

Consider how the mind processes every thought, dream, and fear with equal intensity, regardless of whether they are based on real experiences or are merely figments of our imagination. This phenomenon isn't just a peculiarity of the mind; it's a potent force that shapes our daily lives.

For example, when we lose ourselves in a vivid daydream or engage in intense visualisation, our mind responds as though these scenarios are unfolding in real life. The same areas of the brain get activated, similar emotional responses are triggered, and often, comparable physiological reactions occur as if we were experiencing actual events.

This merging of imagination with reality is a double-edged sword. While it allows us to plan for the future, empathise with others, and solve problems creatively, it also means we might respond to imagined fears and anxieties as though they were immediate, real threats, affecting our mental well-being.

By understanding this unique feature of our mind, we can harness the power of positive thinking. Techniques like visualisation, positive affirmations, and optimistic thinking can cultivate well-being and confidence. Conversely, it's vital to be aware of the pitfalls of negative thought patterns. These patterns can create stress and anxiety over situations that may never occur or aren't as dire as we imagine.

For instance, consider an upcoming presentation. Intellectually, you know it's likely to go well, but if you obsess over potential failures, your mind might experience it multiple times as a disaster, even though the reality is far from it. This process of negative introspection can also occur when we dwell on past events, regretting actions or inactions, thereby feeding into a cycle of anxiety and stress.

THE STRESS BUCKET

In the transformative world of self-help, one powerful metaphor stands out: the stress bucket. This concept, representing the hippocampus in our brain, offers a vivid illustration of how we accumulate and store stress. Imagine each negative thought as a drop of water filling up this imaginary bucket. The idea of the stress bucket helps us understand that handling a certain level of stress and anxiety is completely manageable and, in some cases, even beneficial.

A moderate amount of stress can act as a catalyst, signalling that the task at hand is significant and demands our attention. This could be something like preparing for a job interview or gearing up for a sporting event. It's a kind of stress that heightens our focus and sharpens our performance.

However, the challenge arises when stress accumulates unchecked. Over time, if we don't find ways to manage or release this stress effectively, our stress bucket can start to overflow. This overflow can trigger a cascade of reactions in our brain, including the fight-or-flight response, leading to an overwhelming rush of emotions and physical symptoms.

The stress bucket metaphor helps us recognise that our minds can hold various stressors, from significant life events to minor daily annoyances. It's crucial to understand that both big and small negative thoughts contribute to our overall stress levels.

The key to maintaining our well-being lies in managing the amount of stress in our bucket. By changing how we think about and react to different events and situations, we can prevent our stress bucket from overflowing. This book aims to guide you through practical strategies and thought processes to keep your stress at manageable levels. It's about creating a positive cycle where we control our reactions to stress, rather than letting stress control us. By mastering the art of stress bucket management, we pave the way for a more balanced, fulfilling life.

THE OVERFLOW EFFECT

This overflow is a critical point where our brain perceives imminent danger, triggering an instinctual response. Often, we react with a fight (anxiety) or flight (anger) response.

Imagine this response as setting off an alarm in our body. Our heart rate accelerates, and we are flooded with stress hormones like cortisol and adrenaline. These hormones prime our bodies to either confront or flee from the perceived threat. The result? We find ourselves in a state of heightened anxiety and anger.

When our brains enter this hyper-vigilant mode, constantly on the lookout for danger, it can lead to a cascade of overwhelming emotions. Our thoughts may become irrational, and our behaviours can reflect this disarray. This state of chronic stress is more than just uncomfortable – it can lead to a range of mental health issues, including anxiety disorders, panic attacks, obsessive-compulsive disorder (OCD), and overall low mood.

One significant repercussion of this heightened stress is insomnia. Sleep, which is so crucial for our mental and physical well-being, becomes elusive. This lack of rest only compounds the issues, creating a vicious cycle of stress and sleeplessness.

R.E.M SLEEP (RAPID EYE MOVEMENT)

One of the most powerful tools at our disposal is something we do every night: R.E.M (Rapid Eye Movement) sleep. This phase of sleep offers a remarkable way to empty our metaphorical stress bucket.

Picture this: You've had a challenging day, and an upsetting event keeps replaying in your mind. Despite attempts to shake it off, the emotional residue lingers. But then, something transformative happens as you sleep. During R.E.M sleep, your brain reprocesses these events, converting them from raw, emotional memories into narrative, more manageable ones. This process occurs as we dream, whether we remember the dreams or not, and it helps move these memories from the primitive part of our brain (where they're emotionally charged) to the intellectual part, where we can view them more rationally.

When we wake up after a cycle of R.E.M sleep, we often find that the intensity of our emotions about the previous day's events has diminished. You might still remember the incident, but your emotional response is altered – you might find yourself wondering why you allowed it to upset you so much.

R.E.M sleep is not just for processing daily events; it's crucial for assimilating new information and experiences. However, it's important to note that R.E.M constitutes only about 20% of our sleep cycle. If our stress bucket is too full, it can disrupt this delicate balance. There are two common responses to an overloaded stress bucket:

1. **Interrupted Sleep**: If your mind is overly burdened, it might wake you up abruptly, leaving you wide awake and frustrated. This type of wakefulness is different from being startled awake by an external noise and can often lead to feelings of misery and difficulty returning to sleep.
2. **Exhaustion from Overactive R.E.M**: Sometimes, in an attempt to process excessive stress, we may experience prolonged R.E.M phases. While this might seem helpful, it can

actually lead to exhaustion, leaving us feeling more anxious or depressed, even after a long sleep.

This can create a vicious cycle: the more we sleep (or struggle to sleep), the more items get added to our stress bucket, exacerbating our anxiety and depression. However, once we understand and start reversing this cycle, we begin to see significant improvements in our overall well-being.

Imagine waking up each morning with a cleared stress bucket, ready to face the day without the burdens of unresolved anxiety, anger, or depression.

WHAT CAN WE DO ABOUT IT?

It's enlightening to look back at our early ancestors to understand the roots of our reward system. Early men and women were rewarded for fulfilling key evolutionary roles, such as hunting, gathering, and supporting their families. These activities were crucial for survival, but they also provided intrinsic rewards that went beyond mere sustenance.

What's fascinating is how these activities, especially when done in groups, not only ensured survival but also fostered a sense of community and belonging. This social aspect of early human life was rewarding in itself, as we, as a species, thrive in collaborative environments rather than in isolation.

The rewards our ancestors experienced were multifaceted. They included:

- Enhanced ability to handle daily activities and challenges.
- Improved coping mechanisms for dealing with physical fear.
- Increased bravery, especially when facing threats.
- Alleviation of physical pain, particularly when in the company of others.

Consider the difference in feeling when walking through a dark alley or a forest at night alone versus with company. The presence of others can significantly reduce fear and provide a sense of safety.

These rewards, as we now understand, were the result of chemical responses in the brain. Neurotransmitters like serotonin, often referred to as the 'feel-good hormone', played a significant role. When our brain releases serotonin, we feel happier, braver, and more equipped to handle various situations.

Drawing inspiration from our early ancestors, we can see the importance of engaging in positive interactions, staying active, and maintaining a positive mind-set. These behaviours help stimulate the continuous flow of serotonin, enhancing our mental health and overall well-being.

WHAT STOPS THE FLOW OF SEROTONIN?

At one end of the emotional spectrum, where feelings of misery and depression reside, there's a significant depletion in the production of feel-good chemicals in our brains. These chemicals are essential for maintaining a balanced mood and outlook on life.

Conversely, at the other extreme where anxiety reigns, our bodies produce an excess of stress hormones and adrenaline. These chemicals are incredibly beneficial in situations of acute danger – like encountering a lion in the wild – as they prepare our bodies for a fight or flight response. However, in the context of our daily lives, an overabundance of these stress hormones can be detrimental, leading to a constant state of unease and tension.

The key to shifting away from this anxious state lies in regaining control of our intellectual mind. This process involves reversing the patterns that lead to anxiety. Positive thinking plays a crucial role in this transformation. By consciously adopting a more optimistic mind-set, we can gradually undo the negative patterns associated with depression, anxiety, and anger.

Chapter 5: The Solution-Focused Approach
Principles of Solution-Focused Therapy

Embracing a Future-Oriented Approach

Solution-Focused therapy is a therapeutic approach that emphasises finding solutions in the present and future, rather than delving into problems in the past. It's about building on what's already working and making progress towards desired goals. Here are some of the key principles and techniques of this approach:

1. The 'Miracle Question'

The 'Miracle Question' is a distinctive technique in solution-focused therapy, which is aimed at emphasising solutions and positive change rather than dwelling on problems. Its primary purpose is to help you articulate what your ideal future would look like, serving as a powerful tool for goal-setting and shifting perspectives.

The process begins with envisioning a scenario where a miracle happens overnight, resolving the issues they are facing. You would then describe in detail what this new reality would look like, including how you would feel, act, think, and how others might notice the change. The focus is on concrete, observable changes. For example, if you are dealing with depression, you might imagine feeling more energetic, engaging in hobbies again, or socialising more.

You might then probe further about the impact of these changes on your life, encompassing relationships, work, and overall well-being. This exploration helps you identify specific changes and aspects of this 'miracle' scenario that are already present or achievable in your current life.

This technique is used in individual therapy sessions to help clients focus on their goals and the steps needed to achieve them. It can also be adapted for self-help purposes, such as in journaling prompts or meditation focuses, to clarify personal goals and aspirations. The Miracle Question fosters a sense of hope and possibility, which can be empowering for clients who feel stuck or overwhelmed. It also enhances motivation by visualising a positive future and helps clients recognise their strengths and resources.

However, it usually requires skilful guidance by the therapist to ensure the client remains focused and gains meaningful insight. Balancing the imaginative aspect with realism is crucial to inspire practical change and not just daydreaming.

The Miracle Question is about breaking free from the limitations of current problems and envisioning a brighter, problem-free future, guiding individuals to discover their goals and start thinking about practical ways to make these aspirations a reality.

2. Identifying Exceptions

Identifying exceptions is a crucial principle in solution-focused therapy, which involves exploring the times when the problem you're facing does not occur or is less severe. This technique helps you to uncover periods in your life where the issue you're dealing with is either absent, minimal, or manageable. By recognising these moments, you gain valuable insights into what you're already doing well and how you can replicate or expand on these successful strategies.

When using this principle, you're encouraged to reflect on your recent past and identify instances where the situation was better. For example, if you're dealing with anxiety, you might recall a day when your anxiety was less intrusive. The goal is to analyse what was different about that day - it could be related to your activities, the people you were with, your environment, or even your thought patterns.

The power of identifying exceptions lies in its ability to shift your focus. Instead of concentrating on the problem and what's going wrong, you start to look for possibilities and what's going right. This shift is significant because it helps you realise that the problem is not all-encompassing and that there are moments of relief and success that can be built upon.

This approach is not just about positive thinking; it's a practical way to discover and reinforce effective coping mechanisms that you may already be using unconsciously. By bringing these strategies into your conscious awareness, you can start to use them more deliberately to manage and potentially overcome your challenges.

Furthermore, identifying exceptions can be a source of hope and motivation. It demonstrates that there are times when you are more resourceful and capable than you might typically feel. This recognition can be incredibly empowering, especially when you're feeling stuck or overwhelmed.

In practice, you can use this principle as a self-help tool by regularly reflecting on your days and noting any times when the problem was less impactful. Keeping a journal can be particularly useful for this exercise. Over time, you'll start to notice patterns and strategies that contribute to these better moments, which can then be intentionally incorporated into your daily life to enhance your well-being and resilience.

3. Scaling Questions

Scaling questions are an integral part of solution-focused therapy, designed to assist individuals in evaluating their current state concerning their goals and desired outcomes. This technique involves asking people to rate themselves on an imaginary scale regarding specific aspects of their lives or the problems they are encountering.

Imagine, for instance, being in a therapeutic setting where you're asked, "On a scale from 1 to 10, where 1 is the worst your problem has ever been and 10 is the problem being completely resolved, where would you place yourself right now?" Such a question is instrumental in gauging the severity of the problem from your viewpoint. More importantly, it helps in pinpointing the small, yet significant, steps of progress you've made and what actions are needed to advance further up the scale.

The real benefit of scaling questions is in their capacity to transform abstract concepts or feelings into something more concrete and measurable. You are prompted to consider degrees of change rather than black-and-white absolutes. This approach can be exceptionally beneficial when progress seems slow or difficult to notice, as it allows for a nuanced appreciation of change and improvement.

Beyond merely assessing where you currently stand, scaling questions can also delve into your past successes. A therapist, or you yourself, might reflect, "Can you recall a time when you were lower on the scale? What was different about that period, and what actions or thoughts helped you to move up to where you are now?" This method of questioning serves to remind you of your own agency and capability to effect change, drawing on your previous successes and coping mechanisms.

Scaling questions are not confined to the realms of therapy; they are equally applicable to personal development and self-reflection. They can play a pivotal role in helping you set realistic goals, monitor your progress, and sustain motivation. The act of quantifying progress, even in small increments, allows for the recognition and celebration of achievements, which is vital for maintaining a positive and proactive mind-set in personal growth and problem-solving.

In essence, scaling questions offer a simple yet profound way for you to assess your growth, set meaningful goals, and acknowledge your potential for change and development. They are a versatile and effective instrument in solution-focused therapy, empowering you to view your journey through a lens of progress and possibility.

4. Building on Strengths

Building on strengths is a fundamental aspect of solution-focused therapy, emphasising the recognition and utilisation of a client's inherent strengths and resources. This approach deviates from traditional methods that often concentrate on weaknesses or deficits. Instead, it focuses on identifying and leveraging what you are already doing well to tackle your challenges.

The premise of this approach is rooted in the belief that every individual possesses a set of unique strengths and past successes that can be harnessed to address current problems. By shifting the focus to these strengths, the therapy encourages a more positive and empowering perspective. It helps you see yourself not as someone overwhelmed by problems, but as someone capable of solving them.

In practice, this might involve a therapist asking you to reflect on times in your life when you successfully navigated a difficult situation. The aim is to explore how you achieved this: what personal qualities, skills, or external resources did you draw upon? Understanding these elements gives you a clearer picture of your strengths and how they can be applied to your current circumstances.

This approach is not about ignoring problems or challenges but about approaching them from a position of strength. It's about recognising that you have already shown resilience and capability in various aspects of your life and that these qualities can be instrumental in dealing with present difficulties.

Building on strengths is particularly effective because it creates a sense of competence and confidence. When you focus on what you can do and have done, rather than on what you can't do or haven't done, it changes your self-perception and enhances your belief in your ability to influence your life positively.

In a broader sense, this principle can be applied beyond therapy, in personal development, education, or even in the workplace. It's about cultivating a mind-set that looks for and builds upon the positives, which can lead to more substantial engagement, higher motivation, and better outcomes in various aspects of life.

Overall, the principle of building on strengths in solution-focused therapy offers an optimistic, empowering approach to personal development and problem-solving. It encourages you to recognise and utilise your innate talents and past achievements as tools for overcoming current and future obstacles.

5. Setting Small, Achievable Goals

In solution-focused therapy, one of the key strategies for achieving positive change is the practice of setting small, achievable goals. This approach is based on the understanding that while grand, sweeping goals can often feel overwhelming and out of reach, smaller, more manageable steps can lead to significant and lasting change.

The idea is to break down your larger objectives into smaller, more immediate goals. These goals should be realistic and achievable, creating a sense of accomplishment and momentum as you progress towards your broader aims. For example, if your ultimate goal is to improve your overall physical health, a small, achievable goal might be to start with a 10-minute walk each day, rather than immediately aiming for an hour of strenuous exercise.

Setting small goals has several benefits. Firstly, it makes the process less intimidating. When a goal seems within reach, you're more likely to take the first step. Secondly, each small success builds your confidence. As you meet these mini-goals, you reinforce your belief in your ability to effect change in your life. This growing confidence can then fuel further progress.

Moreover, small goals allow for quicker feedback and adjustment. If a particular approach isn't working, it's easier to tweak and change course when you're dealing with a smaller objective. This flexibility is crucial for maintaining momentum and staying engaged with the process of change.

This method also encourages a focus on the present and the immediate future, which can be more motivating than distant, more abstract goals. It keeps you rooted in the here and now, engaging actively with your current choices and behaviours.

You can apply this strategy in your own life by first identifying a larger goal you wish to achieve. Then, break this goal down into smaller, actionable steps. Set clear, specific mini-goals and establish a timeline for achieving them. Remember to celebrate your successes along the way, no matter how small they may seem. These accomplishments are the building blocks of your larger journey towards change and self-improvement.

In summary, setting small, achievable goals is a powerful approach that can help you make meaningful changes in your life. It brings clarity, focus, and a sense of achievement to the process of personal growth and development.

6. The Language of Change

In solution-focused therapy, a significant emphasis is placed on the language of change. This approach recognises the powerful impact that words and language can have on your mind-set and perception of your situation. By using positive and proactive language, the focus is shifted towards change, possibility, and solutions, steering away from dwelling on problems and limitations.

The language of change involves framing thoughts and conversations in a way that highlights potential, growth, and positive action. This means speaking in terms of what can be done, what is possible, and what the future may hold, rather than what is lacking or problematic. For instance, instead of saying, "I can't deal with this stress," you might reframe it to, "I'm finding ways to manage stress more effectively." This subtle shift in language can significantly alter your perspective, making challenges seem more manageable and less daunting.

This approach encourages you to acknowledge your agency and capability. It's about recognising that while you may not have control over every aspect of a situation, you do have the power to change how you respond to it. The language of change helps you see yourself as an active participant in your journey, rather than a passive victim of circumstances.

Moreover, this kind of language fosters a sense of hope and optimism. By focusing on what can be achieved and the steps you can take, it opens up a realm of possibilities. It helps you envision a positive future and the path towards it, rather than getting stuck in the narrative of the problem.

As you read this and apply it to your life, consider how you describe your challenges and goals. Pay attention to the words you use and how they might be shaping your perception. Try to rephrase negative or limiting statements into ones that reflect action, possibility, and positivity. For example, replace thoughts like "I always fail at this" with "I'm learning and growing from each experience."

In essence, the language of change is a powerful tool in solution-focused therapy and self-help. It's not just about being positive; it's about actively choosing words that steer you towards solutions, empowerment, and growth. By consciously adopting this language, you can start to shift your mind-set and open yourself up to new possibilities and pathways for change.

Empowerment and Future Orientation

A Shift in Perspective

In the journey towards better mental health and personal growth, one of the most transformative steps you can take is shifting your perspective from being problem-focused to becoming solution-focused and future-oriented. This change in mind-set is at the heart of empowerment and is a crucial element in Solution-Focused Hypnotherapy, as well as in your personal development journey.

Traditionally, when we face challenges, our instinct is to dwell deeply on the problems, dissecting their origins and impacts on our lives. While understanding the root of problems is important, an excessive focus on them can keep us anchored in the past, preventing us from moving forward. Solution-Focused Hypnotherapy, and indeed any effective self-help approach, encourages you to redirect your focus. Instead of asking "Why is this happening to me?" the question becomes "What do I want my future to look like, and how can I get there?"

This shift in perspective is incredibly powerful. It moves the spotlight from what's going wrong to what can go right. It's about visualising a future where you've overcome your current challenges and mapping out the steps to reach that future. For instance, rather than spending your energy analysing the causes of your anxiety, you focus on imagining a life where you manage your anxiety effectively and the actionable steps to achieve that.

The impact of this shift cannot be overstated. It opens up a world of possibilities and positive change. When you start looking at your life through a lens of solutions and future potential, you begin to identify opportunities for growth that you might have missed before. This approach instils a sense of hope and control – you realise that while the past is unchangeable, the future is yours to shape.

Moreover, this future-oriented perspective is empowering. It recognises that you have the power to influence your future. Focusing on your goals and the actions you need to take to achieve them moves you from a passive state of experiencing problems to an active state of creating solutions.

As you read this, think about areas in your life where a shift in thinking from problem-focused to solution-focused could make a difference. Reflect on the challenges you face and how envisioning a positive outcome could motivate and guide your actions. What does your desired future look like, and what small steps can you take today towards that future?

In essence, moving from a problem-focused mind-set to a future-oriented, solution-based mind-set isn't just about positive thinking; it's about actively focusing on creating the future you desire. This shift in perspective is a key step in your journey towards personal empowerment and achieving the change you seek in your life.

From Problems to Possibilities

In the realm of self-help and personal development, there's a significant shift occurring in how we approach our challenges and mental health. Traditionally, therapy and mental health care have focused extensively on exploring problems, dissecting their origins, and understanding their impact on our lives. This approach has its value, certainly, as it helps in recognising and understanding the depth of our issues. However, it also has a tendency to anchor us in the past, often binding us to our difficulties and the narratives that we create around them.

Solution-Focused Hypnotherapy offers a refreshing and effective alternative. This approach pivots the conversation and our thought process away from dwelling on problems. Instead, it directs our attention towards solutions, possibilities, and the outcomes we desire. It's a perspective that encourages us not to linger on what has gone wrong or what is missing from our lives, but to focus on what we want to achieve and how we can get there.

This shift from problems to possibilities is not just about avoiding negative thoughts; it's about actively creating a path forward. It involves envisioning a future where you have overcome your current obstacles and are living the life you aspire to. By focusing on solutions and what's possible, you open up a space where change can occur. It's about asking yourself, "What steps can I take to move closer to my goals?" rather than "Why am I stuck with these problems?"

For you, as a reader seeking to enhance your life and overcome challenges, this approach can be incredibly empowering. It moves you out of a passive role where life happens to you, to an active role where you are the creator of your own life. It encourages you to identify your strengths, the resources you have at your disposal, and the small steps you can take to bring about the change you desire.

Consider how this shift in perspective can apply to your own life. Instead of focusing on the issues that weigh you down, try to imagine what your life would look like without these barriers. What does that picture look like, and what practical steps can you take to move towards it? This approach doesn't just create a more positive outlook; it can actively guide you towards making tangible changes.

In summary, moving from a focus on problems to a concentration on possibilities and solutions is a powerful strategy in your personal development journey. It's about changing the way you perceive your challenges and reorienting yourself towards a future filled with potential and growth. This approach is at the heart of Solution-Focused Hypnotherapy and can be a transformative tool in your quest for a more fulfilling life.

The Power of the 'What If'

Imagine for a moment the profound impact of shifting your mind-set from dwelling on "What's wrong with me?" to contemplating "What if things could be better?" This subtle yet powerful change in questioning has the potential to open up a world of possibilities for you. It's a transformative way of thinking that encourages you to envision a future where you have risen above your current challenges and are living the life you truly desire.

Think about it – often, our inner dialogue is filled with self-doubt and negative questioning. We get caught up in analysing our flaws and limitations, which can leave us feeling stuck and hopeless. But what if you redirected that energy? What if you started asking yourself questions that ignite hope and inspire action?

The power of "What if" lies in its ability to shift your focus. Instead of being anchored in the problems of the present or the regrets of the past, this question propels you into the realm of future possibilities. It's about giving yourself permission to dream and to consider a future where things are better, where you've overcome the hurdles that seem insurmountable right now.

This approach doesn't mean ignoring your current struggles or challenges. Instead, it's about changing your perspective on them. By asking "What if things could be better?" you start to look for potential solutions, opportunities for growth, and ways to turn your aspirations into reality.

Envisioning a positive future can be incredibly motivating. It helps you to see beyond your immediate circumstances and realise that there is a path forward. It can also help you identify the steps you need to take to start moving towards that better future. Whether it's improving your mental health, advancing in your career, nurturing your relationships, or any other aspect of your life, starting with the question "What if?" opens up a space for creative problem-solving and strategic planning.

So, as you read this, take a moment to reflect on your own life. What are the areas where you feel stuck or dissatisfied? Now, reframe your thoughts. Instead of focusing on what's wrong or what you lack, ask yourself, "What if things could be better in these areas? What would that look like, and what steps can I take to get there?"

Embracing the power of "What if" is a simple yet profound step you can take on your journey to a more fulfilling life. It's an invitation to dream, to plan, and most importantly, to act. Remember, every great achievement starts with the question of what could be possible.

Creating a Vision for the Future

Creating a vivid and compelling vision of your future is an essential part of your journey towards personal growth and fulfilment. This isn't about indulging in unrealistic fantasies or daydreams. Rather, it's about defining clear, achievable goals that resonate deeply with your values and aspirations. By focusing on what you genuinely want to achieve, instead of what you want to avoid or move away from, you're setting yourself on a positive path of change and growth.

Imagine this process as mapping out a destination for a journey. It's about having a clear picture of where you want to go, what it looks like, and what it feels like to be there. This vision of your future should be as detailed and specific as possible. For instance, if your goal is to improve your career, visualise what your ideal job would entail – the responsibilities you'd have, the environment you'd work in, the kind of colleagues you'd interact with, and even how you'd feel every day going to work.

This vision-setting is powerful because it gives you a concrete destination to aim for. It's not just a vague idea of "better" – it's a specific, tangible picture of what "better" looks like for you. With this clear vision, you can start to identify the steps you need to take to get there. Each goal becomes a milestone on your journey towards this envisioned future.

Remember, the key is to ensure that your vision aligns with your personal values and true aspirations. It's not about what others expect from you or what you think you should want. It's deeply personal and should resonate with who you are and what you genuinely desire.

As you ponder over your vision for the future, consider the aspects of your life that are most important to you. Think about your career, your personal relationships, your health, your hobbies, and interests. What does success and fulfilment look like in each of these areas? Be honest and bold in your vision. This is your life, and the canvas is yours to paint.

In creating this vision, you're doing more than just setting goals. You're charting a course for your future – a future that excites you, motivates you, and is in harmony with your deepest values. So take this moment to reflect on what you truly want, and start to build a vision that will guide you towards a future filled with achievement and personal satisfaction.

Empowerment Through Action

Empowerment is a crucial concept in your journey towards personal growth and self-improvement. It's about recognising and embracing the fact that you have the power to effect change in your life. This empowerment involves a significant shift: moving from a passive state, where you might feel that problems are simply happening to you, to an active state, where you are actively engaged in finding and implementing solutions.

It's important to understand that being empowered doesn't imply that the path ahead will always be easy or straightforward. Challenges and obstacles are an inevitable part of life. However, empowerment means acknowledging that you are not helpless in the face of these challenges. You have choices, you have agency, and you can take steps, however small, towards overcoming the hurdles you encounter.

Consider your current situation. Are there aspects of your life where you feel things are happening to you, and you're merely reacting? Now, think about how you can shift this perspective. How can you take a more active role? This could involve setting goals, making plans, seeking out resources, or simply changing your mind-set from one of passivity to one of proactive engagement.

Empowerment through action is about taking control of your narrative. It's about writing your story, one decision, and one action at a time. It's about not waiting for things to change on their own but instead taking steps, however small, to initiate that change. This approach breeds confidence and a sense of accomplishment, fuelling further action and more significant change.

Remember, every great journey begins with a single step. Your empowerment lies in recognising that you have the strength and capability to take that step and then the next one. While the road may not always be smooth, your proactive stance ensures that you are not just a spectator in your life but the driver, steering towards your goals and aspirations.

So, take a moment to reflect on where you stand today. Where can you take action, however small, to make a change? Embrace the understanding that you are capable and powerful in your life's journey. Your empowerment comes from this recognition and the actions you take, leading to a fulfilling and purpose-driven life.

Building on Successes

A vital aspect of your journey towards personal growth and achievement is the practice of building on your successes. This approach focuses on identifying and leveraging the strengths and successes you already have, no matter how small they may seem. Each success you experience, every milestone you reach, is a step forward towards your larger goals.

Consider for a moment the successes you've had in your life, even the seemingly insignificant ones. These could be anything from completing a task you've been postponing, making progress in a personal hobby, or successfully handling a difficult conversation. Recognising and valuing these successes is not just about giving yourself a pat on the back. It's about understanding that each of these achievements is a building block, a concrete demonstration of your ability to overcome challenges and move forward.

This practice of building on successes is crucial because it shifts your focus from what you haven't achieved to what you have. It changes the narrative from one of deficiency to one of capability. This shift in perspective can be incredibly empowering. It reminds you that you have a history of success, however small, and that you can draw on this history to face current and future challenges.

The act of acknowledging and celebrating your successes also serves as a reinforcement of your abilities. It boosts your confidence and motivates you to take on new challenges. It helps you see that progress, even in small increments, is still progress. It's a tangible reminder that you are moving closer to your desired future with every success you achieve.

So, as you move forward in your personal development, make it a habit to recognise and build upon your successes. Take time to reflect on what you've accomplished and how it has contributed to your growth. Celebrate these successes, learn from them, and use them as a foundation for your next steps.

Remember, your journey towards your goals is made up of many small steps. Each success, no matter its size, is a part of that journey. By building on these successes, you reinforce your path towards a brighter, more accomplished future. You have a track record of success – use it as a springboard to achieve even more.

Looking Forward

As we continue our journey through *MINDPLAN*, we're going to dive deeper into practical ways you can apply these empowering principles in your own life. Together, we'll explore strategies and exercises specifically designed to help shift your focus from dwelling on problems to identifying and working toward solutions. This shift is key to empowering you to actively create a future that aligns with your deepest aspirations and goals.

Imagine being equipped with tools and techniques that transform the way you approach challenges, turning obstacles into stepping stones toward your success. That's exactly what we'll be focusing on. Each strategy and exercise is aimed at enhancing your ability to think creatively, solve problems effectively, and make decisions that propel you towards the life you want to live.

Think of these upcoming chapters as a workshop where you'll be actively involved in shaping your future. You'll learn how to set clear, achievable goals and break them down into manageable steps. We'll also delve into the power of positive thinking and how to harness your inner strengths and successes to overcome challenges.

One of the most exciting aspects of this journey is that you'll not only be learning these strategies but also applying them in real-time to your life. This practical application is what makes *MINDPLAN* a truly dynamic and interactive experience. You'll have the chance to practice new ways of thinking and acting, experiment with different approaches to problem-solving, and see first-hand how small changes can lead to significant results.

As you progress through *MINDPLAN*, remember that this journey is about you. It's about unlocking your potential, realising your capabilities, and crafting a life that's not only fulfilling but also truly yours. The power to change, grow, and achieve lies within you, and *MINDPLAN* is here to help you unleash that power.

So, look forward to this journey with excitement and an open mind. The path ahead is filled with possibilities and opportunities for growth. With each step, you'll be moving closer to creating a future that resonates with your aspirations, a future where your dreams and goals are not just possibilities but realities.

Case Studies: Success Stories with Solution-Focused Therapy

Transformations Through Focus and Empowerment

To illustrate the impact of a solution-focused approach, let's explore real-life case studies. These stories highlight how shifting from a problem-centric view to a solution-oriented mind-set can lead to significant positive changes.

Case Study 1: Overcoming Anxiety - The Story of Emma

Background:

Emma, with her creative flair, excelled in her role as a graphic designer. However, her severe anxiety, particularly in social contexts, cast a shadow over her professional and personal life. She often found herself overwhelmed by the fear of being judged by others, which led her to avoid team meetings, social gatherings, and even regular interactions with colleagues. This not only hindered her professional growth but also led her into a state of isolation, affecting her overall well-being.

Solution-Focused Therapy Approach:

Visioning Exercise: Rather than delving deep into the origins of Emma's anxiety, her therapist started with a visioning exercise. Emma was encouraged to envision a version of her life where anxiety didn't control her social interactions. This exercise helped her to see the possibility of change and what her life could look like.

Identifying Exceptions: Emma, through guided conversations, identified moments when her anxiety felt manageable. These included times when she was deeply engaged in her design work or when she was in smaller, more intimate groups. Understanding these exceptions provided clues to situations where Emma felt more at ease.

Setting Small Goals: With her therapist's guidance, Emma set small, achievable goals. Initially, these goals were as simple as exchanging morning greetings with a colleague or commenting on a discussion during a team meeting. These goals were designed to gradually expose her to social interactions in a controlled and manageable way.

Progress Tracking: Emma and her therapist regularly reviewed her progress, celebrating even minor achievements and adjusting the goals as needed. This ongoing evaluation helped Emma recognise her growth and adapt her strategies.

Outcome:

Shift in Focus: Over time, Emma's focus shifted from the intensity of her anxiety to her successes in social situations, no matter how small. This shift was crucial as it reinforced a positive self-perception and reduced the overwhelming nature of her anxiety.

Building Confidence: Each small victory, like initiating a conversation or participating in a meeting, significantly boosted Emma's confidence. She gradually started to engage more with her colleagues and even attended some social events, initially for short durations.

Improved Quality of Life: As Emma continued to work on her goals, she noticed a considerable improvement in her comfort level in social settings. Her enhanced confidence reflected in her professional life too, where she started to contribute more actively in team projects and discussions.

Long-term Change: Emma's journey wasn't without its challenges, but the consistent application of solution-focused strategies equipped her with tools to manage her anxiety effectively. Over time, these strategies led to a sustained improvement in her quality of life, both professionally and personally.

Case Study 2: Breaking Free from Depression - The Journey of Michael

Background:

Michael, a 45-year-old teacher, found himself grappling with the debilitating effects of chronic depression. His condition manifested as a pervasive sense of hopelessness, a cycle of negative thoughts, and a profound lack of motivation, which severely impacted his professional and personal life.

Solution-Focused Therapy Approach:

Identifying Better Moments: During his therapy sessions, Michael and his therapist worked on identifying occasions when his depressive symptoms were less intense. This exercise helped Michael recognise that there were indeed times when he experienced some relief from his depressive state, even if they were brief.

Understanding Contributing Factors: Through thoughtful reflection and guidance, Michael explored what was different about these better moments. He realised that certain activities, like spending time in nature or engaging in light physical activity, often coincided with these instances of reduced symptoms.

Envisioning a Depression-Free Future: Michael was encouraged to imagine what his life would look like without the weight of depression. This exercise was not about creating an unrealistically perfect vision but about picturing a realistic, attainable state where he felt better and more in control.

Setting Small, Achievable Goals: Michael started setting small, achievable goals. These included incorporating a daily walk into his routine and reconnecting with an old hobby that he had abandoned due to his depression. These goals were tailored to be manageable and not overwhelming, allowing Michael to build up his sense of accomplishment gradually.

Outcome:

Shift in Perspective: As Michael started to focus on his set goals and celebrated each small achievement, he noticed a gradual shift in his perspective. He began to feel more in control of his life, which was a stark contrast to the helplessness that often accompanies depression.

Reduced Frequency of Depressive Episodes: With consistent effort and the application of solution-focused strategies, Michael experienced a reduction in the frequency and intensity of his depressive episodes. He found that engaging in activities and achieving his goals gave him a sense of purpose and satisfaction.

Improved Overall Mood and Outlook: Over time, these small steps culminated in significant improvements in Michael's mood and general outlook on life. He reported feeling more optimistic about the future and found himself better equipped to manage his depressive symptoms.

Case Study 3: Managing Stress - Sarah's Transformation

Background:

Sarah, a 38-year-old mother of two, found herself in a relentless cycle of stress due to her demanding job and the responsibilities of parenting. This constant state of overwhelm left her feeling perpetually exhausted and irritable, affecting both her professional efficiency and her family life.

Solution-Focused Therapy Approach:

Envisioning a Stress-Free Day: In her therapy sessions, Sarah was encouraged to describe what a typical day without stress would look like for her. This exercise wasn't about creating an idealistic, problem-free scenario but rather about envisioning a more balanced and manageable day-to-day life.

Identifying Less Stressful Times: Sarah reflected on times when she felt less burdened by stress. By recognising these instances, she began to understand what factors contributed to her feeling more relaxed and in control.

Developing Practical Strategies: Based on these insights, Sarah and her therapist worked together to develop practical strategies to replicate those stress-reducing conditions more frequently. This involved setting achievable and realistic goals.

Setting Achievable Goals: One of Sarah's goals was to delegate more tasks at work. She realised that trying to handle everything herself was a significant source of stress. Another goal was to schedule regular 'me time' to recharge, something she had neglected in her busy schedule.

Outcome:

Effective Stress Management: By focusing on specific solutions and achievable goals, Sarah was able to manage her stress more effectively. She learned the importance of delegating tasks and prioritising her well-being, which significantly reduced her overall stress levels.

Empowerment and Improved Capability: This solution-focused approach empowered Sarah. She felt more capable of handling her responsibilities both at work and home. Recognising that she had the power to influence her circumstances positively was a crucial factor in her transformation.

Decreased Stress Levels: As Sarah implemented these strategies, she noticed a marked decrease in her stress levels. She reported feeling more balanced, happier, and more present both in her professional role and with her family.

Conclusion

As we reflect on the journeys of Emma, Michael, and Sarah, it's clear that their stories are more than just individual tales of overcoming anxiety, depression, and stress. They are powerful illustrations of how solution-focused approaches can bring about profound changes in mental well-being, regardless of the challenges one faces. These case studies offer valuable insights that you can apply to your own life.

Emma's story teaches us about the power of confronting anxiety, not by delving deep into its roots, but by envisioning a life free from its crippling hold. Her experience shows how setting small, achievable goals can gradually build the confidence needed to navigate social situations more comfortably. If you're struggling with anxiety, remember that small steps can lead to significant changes.

Michael's experience with chronic depression highlights the importance of recognising moments of relief and using them as a foundation for building a more positive future. By setting attainable goals and acknowledging every small victory, he was able to shift his perspective and reduce the frequency of his depressive episodes. This approach can be a beacon of hope if you're facing similar challenges.

Sarah's transformation underlines the significance of managing stress through practical strategies. By identifying less stressful times and incorporating achievable goals like delegating tasks and scheduling 'me time,' she was able to regain control over her life. Her story is a reminder that even amidst the chaos of juggling multiple responsibilities, finding balance and reducing stress is possible.

These stories collectively underscore a crucial message: You have the power to change your narrative. Whether it's anxiety, depression, stress, or any other mental health challenge, adopting a solution-focused approach can open up a path towards a more fulfilling and balanced life. It encourages you to focus on possibilities, leverage your strengths, and take proactive steps towards your desired future.

As you reflect on these stories, consider how you can apply these lessons to your own life. Remember, the journey towards better mental health is not linear and requires patience, persistence, and a willingness to celebrate each small step of progress. Emma, Michael, and Sarah's stories are testaments to the resilience of the human spirit and the transformative power of adopting a solution-focused mind-set. Your journey, too, can lead to profound personal growth and a greater sense of well-being.

Chapter 6: The Digital Age and Mental Health
Navigating the Impact of Technology

In an era where our lives are intricately woven with digital threads, understanding the impact of technology on our mental health is more crucial than ever. Before reading this, you might have been holding a smartphone, or perhaps in front of a computer screen.

Technology, an integral part of your daily routine, brings a world of information to your fingertips and connects you to people thousands of miles away. Yet, have you ever paused to consider how these digital interactions are influencing your mental well-being?

This chapter is dedicated to you – to help you navigate the complexities of the digital age while prioritising your mental health.

Together, we'll explore the dual nature of technology: its benefits and its challenges. Most importantly, I'll guide you through practical strategies to create a balanced relationship with technology, one that nurtures rather than depletes your mental health.

The Double-Edged Sword of Technology

The Bright Side of the Screen

Technology, in its myriad forms, has undeniably made our lives more connected and convenient. Think about the ease of online shopping, the instant access to news, or the joy of video-calling a loved one who's miles away. These are just a few examples of how technology has enriched our lives, providing comfort and connection in an increasingly fast-paced world.

The Shadow Behind the Light

While the digital age has brought unprecedented access and connectivity, it's not without its darker side. One significant issue is the constant barrage of notifications, contributing to information overload and heightening stress levels. Moreover, the curated realities on social media platforms can foster a world of unrealistic expectations and pressures, leading users to compare their lives unfavourably with those of others.

Another serious concern in this digital landscape is online bullying (or cyber bullying). The anonymity and reach of the internet can sometimes embolden individuals to engage in harmful behaviours, targeting others with negative, often aggressive, comments or messages. This can have profound effects on mental health, contributing to anxiety, depression, and a sense of isolation.

Additionally, the addictive nature of digital devices can lead to prolonged screen time. This not only affects physical health, such as eye strain and poor sleep patterns, but can also significantly impact mental well-being. The more time spent on these devices, the less time is available for meaningful, real-world interactions and activities that are crucial for mental wellness.

The digital age, therefore, presents a complex array of challenges that need to be navigated with awareness and care to protect our mental well-being.

Understanding the Impact on Mental Health

The Invisible Burden

In the digital world, mental health challenges often manifest subtly. You might feel a pang of loneliness scrolling through photos of friends on social media or experience a wave of anxiety from a flood of work emails. These experiences are common in our digitally saturated lives.

Constant connectivity can lead to a state of perpetual alertness. The never-ending stream of notifications and emails can create an underlying sense of anxiety, as you feel pressured to always be "on" and responsive.

Social media platforms, while connecting us with others, can also become a source of comparison and discontent. The habit of comparing your real life with others' curated online personas can foster feelings of inadequacy and depression.

Ironically, despite being more connected than ever, many of us feel more isolated than ever. Digital interactions, while valuable, can't fully replace the emotional depth and satisfaction of face-to-face connections. We need positive interactions to help produce serotonin.

Strategies for Healthy Digital Habits

Setting Boundaries with Technology

Embarking on the journey to healthier digital habits begins with a crucial step: setting clear and firm boundaries. It's about taking control and making intentional choices regarding when, where, and how you engage with technology. This proactive approach not only helps in managing screen time but also reinstates a sense of personal space, essential for mental tranquillity.

Imagine a world where you're not constantly tethered to your devices. Designate specific times during your day for a digital rest. This could be during family meals, allowing you to fully engage and connect with loved ones, or perhaps the last hour before bedtime, creating a calm and technology-free zone that promotes better sleep.

Consider setting aside portions of your weekend as 'offline' time, dedicating these moments to hobbies and activities that you enjoy in the physical world. This practice isn't just about reducing screen time; it's a reclamation of your time, a statement that you are more than the sum of your digital interactions.

In a world buzzing with alerts and updates, managing your notifications can feel like navigating a digital jungle. Take charge of this chaos by turning off non-essential alerts. This means evaluating each app and deciding whether its notifications deserve your immediate attention.

For your peace of mind, designate specific times to check emails or messages. You might decide to review emails during a set time in the morning and then again in the afternoon, thereby avoiding the constant interruption of your day and preserving your focus and productivity. This mindful approach to notifications helps cultivate a more serene digital environment, reducing the stress and anxiety often associated with relentless digital demands.

Incorporating these practices into your daily routine marks the beginning of a healthier, more balanced relationship with technology.

It's about nurturing a space where technology serves you, not the other way around. By setting these boundaries, you're taking an important step towards safeguarding your mental health and reclaiming your right to be present in your own life.

Mindful Usage of Social Media

Transforming your social media experience from a potential stressor to a source of joy and connection begins with mindfulness. Mindful social media usage is about being conscious and intentional with your engagement. It's not just the time you spend on these platforms, but the quality and purpose of that time which truly matters.

Venture into your social media world with a sense of purpose. Actively choose to follow accounts that spark joy, inspire creativity, or educate you. Whether it's accounts that share breath-taking nature photography, uplifting stories, educational content, or simply friends and family who bring a smile to your face, curate your feed to be a source of positivity.

When you engage with social media, do it with intention. Leave comments that are meaningful, share content that resonates with you, and engage in ways that enrich your experience. This active, purposeful engagement transforms your social media from a passive scrolling marathon into a selective journey of meaningful interaction.

As you navigate through your feeds, practice mindfulness. Be aware of how different posts make you feel. If certain content consistently leaves you feeling inadequate, anxious, or unhappy, it might be time to reconsider whether those accounts serve your well-being. Remember, your mental space is precious, and what you consume digitally should respect and uplift that space.

Social media often showcases the highlight reels of people's lives, carefully curated and edited. It's important to gently remind yourself that these snippets do not represent the full reality of someone's life. Everyone has challenges and struggles, despite what their online persona might portray. By consciously separating the online image from the full spectrum of real life, you reduce the risk of unrealistic comparisons that can lead to feelings of inadequacy or envy. This perspective is crucial in maintaining a healthy and realistic view of your own life in relation to what you see online.

Develop your digital literacy by understanding the mechanisms behind social media - the algorithms designed to keep you engaged and the tactics used for attention. Equally, nurture your emotional intelligence to better understand and manage your reactions to social media content. This combination of digital savvy and emotional understanding forms a shield, protecting you from the negative impacts of social media use.

Incorporating these mindful practices into your social media use can significantly alter your digital experience, steering it towards a more positive and fulfilling part of your life. It's about making social media a tool for connection and inspiration, not a battleground for your self-esteem.

Embracing Digital Detox and Unplugging

In our hyper-connected world, the idea of disconnecting from digital devices might seem daunting, yet it is a powerful tool for rejuvenating your mental well-being. Regular digital detoxes –

periods when you intentionally step away from all your screens –
can bring a refreshing sense of balance and peace to your life.

Choose a timeframe for your digital detox that feels realistic and
beneficial. It could be a few hours each day, a full day over the
weekend, or even a week-long break if you're feeling adventurous.
During this time, commit to turning off your smartphones, tablets,
laptops, and even avoiding television. Inform your friends, family,
or colleagues about your digital detox plan, so they understand
and respect your digital boundaries during this period.

Rediscovering Offline Activities: The absence of digital
distractions opens up a world of possibilities for engaging in offline
activities that nourish your soul. Rekindle your love for reading
physical books, delve into creative pursuits like painting or writing,
or start a DIY project. These activities not only provide a break
from screen time but also stimulate your creativity and passion.

Incorporating physical exercise, like going to the gym, elevates this
practice to a new level of well-being. Plan to include gym sessions
or other forms of physical exercise during your digital detox
periods. Whether it's a vigorous workout at the gym, a yoga
session, or a brisk walk, physical activity is a potent enhancer of
mental health. When you swap screen time for sweat time, you're
not only giving your eyes a rest but also boosting your body's
endorphin levels, making you feel happier.

Regular exercise has been shown to significantly reduce
symptoms of anxiety and depression. It promotes the release of
neurotransmitters like serotonin and dopamine, which play a key
role in regulating mood and combating stress. Moreover, engaging
in physical activities, especially in a gym setting, can provide a
sense of routine, structure, and achievement – all of which are
beneficial for mental clarity and self-esteem.

Going to the gym or joining group fitness classes can also foster a
sense of community. Social interactions, even when non-verbal,
during a workout can combat feelings of loneliness and isolation.
The shared experience of exercise not only motivates but also

connects you with others who are prioritising their health and well-being.

Regular physical activity, particularly activities that increase your heart rate, not only benefits the body but also the mind. Exercise has been shown to improve cognitive functions, enhance concentration, and even stimulate the growth of new brain cells. This mental sharpness is a valuable counterbalance to the often foggy, distracted state induced by excessive screen time.

Incorporating gym time or other physical exercises into your routine, especially during periods of digital detox, provides several benefits. It not only supports your physical health and improves your body shape and overall appearance, but also plays a crucial role in maintaining and improving your mental well-being. By choosing to unplug and engage in physical activity, you're making a powerful statement about the importance of your health in both the digital and physical realms.

Use this digital-free time to reconnect with loved ones face-to-face. Organise a family game night, a coffee date with a friend, or a community event. Similarly, immerse yourself in the natural world. Whether it's a leisurely walk in the park, a hike in the woods, or a day spent gardening, nature has a calming effect on the mind and helps ground you in the present moment.

Digital detox periods are perfect for practicing mindfulness and engaging in self-reflection. Without the constant buzz of notifications, you can focus better on meditation or yoga, allowing for a deeper connection with your inner self. These moments of quiet introspection are invaluable for mental clarity and emotional well-being.

In the silence of a digital detox, embrace the quietude. It's in these moments of stillness that you often find clarity and a renewed sense of purpose. Being with your thoughts, free from digital interruptions, can be a profound experience, offering insights into your desires, dreams, and the direction you wish your life to take.

By regularly incorporating digital detoxes into your routine, you create an essential space for personal growth, mental rest, and a deeper connection with the world around you. It's a powerful statement in reclaiming your time and attention, ensuring that your life, not your devices, dictates your experiences.

Harnessing Technology for Mental Wellness

Technology as a Tool for Well-being

While technology can pose challenges to mental health, it also offers remarkable tools to enhance it. By choosing the right digital resources, you can turn your devices into allies for your mental well-being.

There are plenty of Apps that offer guided meditation, mindfulness exercises and access to professional counselling. These can be particularly useful for managing stress, improving sleep and making mental health support more accessible and convenient.

Tools that track your digital usage emerge as invaluable allies. These tools, often available as apps or built-in features in your devices, offer a window into your digital habits, shining a light on how much time you actually spend on various apps and websites.

By employing these tracking tools, you receive concrete data on your screen time, most frequented apps, and even the number of times you pick up your phone. This level of insight is often surprising and can be a real eye-opener. It's not uncommon to underestimate our digital usage, and these tools present the facts in a clear, unambiguous manner.

You might notice that your screen time spikes during certain hours of the day or when you engage in specific activities. Recognising these patterns is the first step in understanding the emotional or situational triggers that drive you to reach for your device. This awareness is crucial for making conscious changes to your digital habits.

Once you're aware of your current digital habits, these tools can assist you in setting realistic goals for reducing screen time. Whether it's cutting down on social media use, managing your email checking habits, or reducing overall screen time, you can use these tools to track your progress. Many apps offer features like setting daily limits for specific apps, reminding you to take screen breaks, or providing weekly reports on your usage.

The data provided by these tools empowers you to take control, helping you to break free from unintended patterns of excessive digital consumption.

Over time, by consistently using these tracking tools and adjusting your habits, you'll likely notice an improvement in your overall digital well-being. Reduced screen time often correlates with better sleep, improved focus, and a greater sense of control over your digital life.

Incorporating digital usage tracking tools into your routine is more than just a measure of how much you use your devices. It's a step towards deeper self-awareness and a more mindful approach to technology, paving the way for a healthier, more balanced digital life.

Integrating Technology with Mental Health Practices

Use technology to complement physical activities. For example, fitness apps can enhance your exercise routine, and meditation apps can aid your mindfulness practice.

Engage with online support groups or forums that focus on mental health. These can provide a sense of community and shared understanding.

Chapter 7: Setting Goals for Mental Health

Goal-Setting Techniques: Pathways to Progress

Crafting a Roadmap for Success

Effective goal setting is a cornerstone of the solution-focused approach. It transforms vague aspirations into tangible targets, providing clear direction and motivation. Let's explore three powerful goal-setting techniques: SMART goals, vision boards, and journaling.

1. SMART Goals: Specific, Measurable, Achievable, Relevant, Time-bound

The SMART framework turns nebulous dreams into achievable goals. Here's how it works:

- **Specific**: Define your goal with clarity. Instead of saying, "I want to be healthier," say, "I want to exercise three times a week."
- **Measurable**: Ensure you can track your progress. If your goal is to reduce stress, a measurable aspect could be, "I will practice 10 minutes of mindfulness daily."
- **Achievable**: Set goals that are realistic and attainable. Overly ambitious goals can lead to disappointment.
- **Relevant**: Choose goals that align with your values and long-term objectives.
- **Time-bound**: Set a deadline to create a sense of urgency and focus. For instance, "I will complete a 5K run in three months."

2. Vision Boards: Visualising Success

A vision board is a collage of images, words, and items that represent your goals and dreams. The process of creating a vision board can be a powerful exercise in clarifying and visualising your aspirations. Place your vision board somewhere you can see it daily to keep your goals top of mind and stir positive emotions.

3. Journaling: Reflection and Clarity

Journaling is a profound way to explore your thoughts, feelings, and aspirations. It can help in setting and refining goals. Consider these journaling prompts:

- "What would my ideal day look like?"
- "What are three things I am most passionate about?"
- "What small step can I take today towards my goal?"

Through regular journaling, you can track your progress, reflect on your experiences, and adjust your goals as needed.

Overcoming Obstacles: Navigating Challenges in Goal Setting

Tackling the Roadblocks on Your Path to Success

Setting goals is a vital step towards change, but it's not without its challenges. Understanding and overcoming these obstacles can make your journey towards achieving your goals smoother and more effective.

1. Lack of Clarity: Defining Your True Goals

"A goal properly set is halfway reached." – Zig Ziglar

In the journey of self-improvement, many of us face the formidable challenge of goal ambiguity. It's like setting sail without knowing your destination. You might wish for a happier life or dream of personal enhancement, but these aspirations, as noble as they are, resemble a ship lost in the fog – directionless and uncertain.

Imagine your goal is to "be happier" or "improve your life." These objectives, while admirable, are like clouds in the sky — beautiful yet without form. They lack the specificity and clarity needed to inspire action. Without a clear destination, how can you chart a course?

The key to overcoming this hurdle lies in the art of refining your goals. Consider your objectives as raw diamonds, which, when precisely cut, reveal their true brilliance.

Interrogate Your Ambitions: Begin by asking yourself probing questions. What does "happiness" really mean to you? Is it financial stability, a loving relationship, or a fulfilling career? When you say you want to "improve your life," what areas are you thinking of? Health, knowledge, spirituality?

Break It Down: Once you have a clearer picture, start dissecting these broad goals into smaller, actionable objectives. For instance, if happiness to you means being physically fit, set a goal to exercise three times a week. If it's about learning, commit to reading a book a month.

Embrace Specificity: Be as detailed as possible. Instead of saying, "I want to be healthier," say, "I want to reduce my sugar intake to less than 35 grams a day." Specific goals are measurable, and what gets measured, gets managed.

Set Milestones: Create short-term targets leading up to your main goal. These are like signposts along the road, guiding you and providing a sense of accomplishment as you progress.

Visualise Success: Regularly visualise yourself achieving these goals. This mental rehearsal primes your brain for success and strengthens your commitment.

Flexibility and Adaptation: Be prepared to modify your goals as you evolve. The path to self-improvement is not rigid; it's a river that flows, adapting to the landscape of your life.

In conclusion, the journey to achieving your goals begins with a clear map. By defining what exactly you wish to achieve, you transform vague dreams into attainable objectives. Remember, in the words of the ancient philosopher Seneca, "If one does not know to which port one is sailing, no wind is favourable."

2. Overwhelm: Too Many Goals at Once

"You can do anything, but not everything." – David Allen

The quest for self-improvement often leads us to a crossroads, scattered with numerous paths and endless possibilities. It's tempting to embark on all journeys at once, setting a multitude of goals. However, this eagerness can soon transform into a labyrinth of overwhelm, leaving us stranded in the thicket of our ambitions.

Imagine your goals as seeds you wish to plant in the garden of your life. Planting too many seeds in a small patch not only stifles growth but also leads to a tangled mess where none can thrive. Similarly, setting too many goals, or goals that are too ambitious, can overwhelm your mental and emotional resources, leading to frustration and a sense of inadequacy.

The antidote to this sense of overwhelm lies in the ancient art of prioritisation – choosing which seeds to nurture first.

Assess and Filter: Begin by evaluating your goals. Which ones align most closely with your core values and long-term vision? These are the seeds to water first.

Embrace Sequential Success: Instead of juggling multiple goals, focus on one or two that are most important. Success in these areas will not only boost your confidence but also create a domino effect, paving the way to achieve other objectives.

Set Realistic Timelines: Understand that Rome wasn't built in a day. Set realistic timelines for your goals. This prevents the rush and pressure that accompany unrealistic expectations.

Celebrate Small Wins: Acknowledge and celebrate each milestone. These small victories are the nourishment for your motivation.

Learn to Say No: Sometimes, the power of progress lies in saying no to tasks or goals that do not align with your primary objectives. This isn't giving up; it's strategic focus.

Reassess Regularly: Periodically step back to reassess your priorities. Life is dynamic, and so are your goals. Flexibility in your approach allows you to adapt and thrive.

Seek Support: Remember, it's okay to ask for help. Whether it's advice from a mentor or support from loved ones, shared burdens are lighter.

In conclusion, while it's tempting to chase after every goal that sparkles, remember that focus is the compass that guides you to your treasure. Prioritise, take deliberate steps, and watch as each small victory leads you closer to the fulfilment of your dreams.

3. Motivation: Keeping the Fire Burning

"Motivation is what gets you started. Habit is what keeps you going." – Jim Rohn

Embarking on the journey of achieving your goals is akin to lighting a fire within yourself. This fire represents your motivation – a powerful force that propels you forward. Yet, as the journey unfolds, especially when the path gets steep or the weather turns stormy, keeping this flame alive becomes a challenge of its own.

Imagine your motivation as a campfire in the wilderness of your ambitions. At times, the fire burns brightly, filling you with energy and drive. But there are moments when the flames dwindle, dimmed by slow progress or unexpected setbacks. This is a natural part of any journey, yet it's in these moments that many lose their way.

The key to maintaining your motivation lies not in avoiding these low moments, but in knowing how to reignite your fire during them.

Hold onto Your Vision: Always keep your ultimate vision at the forefront of your mind. This vision is your north star, guiding you through dark and uncertain times. Remind yourself why these goals are important to you and what achieving them will mean for your life.

Celebrate Every Step: No victory is too small to celebrate. Each step forward, no matter how minor it may seem, is a progression towards your goal. These small victories are the sparks that keep your motivational fire burning.

Craft a Motivation Ecosystem: Surround yourself with reminders of your goals and sources of inspiration. Whether it's motivational quotes, a vision board, or stories of those who have walked similar paths, create an environment that fuels your drive.

Embrace the Power of Routine: Build routines and habits that support your goals. When motivation wanes, let these habits carry you forward. The discipline of routine is a powerful force when motivation is low.

Connect with Like-Minded Individuals: Join a community of people who share similar goals. Their energy and progress can be infectious, reigniting your own motivation.

Reflect and Recharge: Regularly take time to reflect on your journey. Recognise how far you've come and allow yourself time to recharge. Rest is not a retreat but a preparation for the next surge forward.

Adjust and Adapt: Be flexible in your approach. If a particular strategy isn't working, be willing to adjust your tactics. Adaptability is a key component of sustained motivation.

In conclusion, the flame of motivation, like any fire, needs constant tending. By keeping your vision clear, celebrating every milestone, and embedding your goals into your daily life, you ensure that this fire burns steadily, illuminating your path to success.

4. Fear of Failure: The Paralysis of Perfectionism

"I have not failed. I've just found 10,000 ways that won't work." –
Thomas Edison

In the odyssey of self-improvement, one of the most formidable adversaries we encounter is the fear of failure. It lurks in the shadows of our aspirations, often dressed as a relentless pursuit of perfection. This fear can paralyse us, leading to procrastination and sometimes, to abandoning the journey of goal-setting altogether.

Imagine standing at the edge of a cliff, your dreams on the other side. The fear of falling – of failing – chains your feet, preventing you from taking the leap. This paralysis stems from a belief that failure is a mark of personal inadequacy, a blemish on one's worth.

The key to breaking free from these chains lies in adopting a growth mind-set, a perspective that views challenges as opportunities and setbacks as stepping stones.

Redefine Failure: Understand that failure is not a reflection of your worth but a natural part of the learning process. It's a teacher, not a judge.

Cultivate a Growth Mind-set: Embrace the belief that abilities and intelligence can be developed. Each attempt, successful or not, is a step towards growth.

Celebrate the Process, Not Just the Outcome: Shift your focus from the end result to the journey of getting there. Recognise the value in the effort, the learning, and the experience.

Embrace Imperfection: Let go of the need for everything to be perfect. Perfection is an illusion; progress is real and tangible.

Learn from Setbacks: Analyse your setbacks and extract lessons from them. What can they teach you? How can they help you grow?

Visualise Success and Failure: Imagine both successful outcomes and potential failures. By visualising failure, you demystify it and reduce its power to paralyse.

Create a Supportive Environment: Surround yourself with people who encourage your growth and understand that setbacks are part of the process.

Set Realistic Expectations: Be honest with yourself about what you can achieve. Unrealistic expectations can amplify the fear of failure.

Start Small: Begin with smaller, manageable goals. Achieving these can build your confidence and resilience.

In conclusion, by embracing a growth mind-set and viewing every step as a valuable part of your journey, you transform the fear of failure into a catalyst for growth. Remember, in the pursuit of your dreams, it's not about avoiding the falls; it's about learning how to get back up with grace and wisdom.

5. Lack of Accountability: Staying on Track

"Accountability breeds response-ability." – Stephen Covey

Embarking on a journey of personal growth and goal achievement is akin to navigating the vast ocean of possibilities. In such a journey, accountability serves as your anchor, ensuring you don't drift away from your chosen path. Without this anchor, it's all too easy to lose sight of your destination or be swayed by the currents of distraction and procrastination.

Imagine setting sail towards your dream island. Without regular checks on your compass and map, you might find yourself off course or even going in circles. Similarly, in the pursuit of goals, lacking accountability can lead to a gradual slackening in efforts, where days slip by unnoticed, and intentions remain just that – intentions.

To stay true to your course, you must create a system of accountability – a compass and map for your journey.

Choose Your Accountability Partners Wisely: Share your goals with someone you trust – a friend, family member, or a mentor. Choose someone who understands your aspirations and is committed to seeing you succeed.

Regular Check-ins: Establish a routine of regular check-ins with your accountability partner. These check-ins serve as waypoints, ensuring you're on the right track and providing an opportunity for course correction if needed.

Be Transparent: Be open and honest about your progress and challenges. The purpose of accountability is not to showcase perfection, but to face up to realities and find ways to overcome them.

Join a Support Group: Consider joining a support group with similar goals. These groups offer not just accountability, but also camaraderie and shared wisdom.

Document Your Journey: Keep a journal or log of your progress. Documenting your journey not only serves as a record of your efforts but also helps in self-reflection.

Embrace Technology: Utilise apps and digital tools designed for goal tracking and accountability. These tools can provide reminders, motivational prompts, and track your progress.

Set Clear Expectations: Be clear about what you expect from your accountability partner and what they can expect from you. This mutual understanding is crucial for effective accountability.

Reward Progress: Celebrate milestones, no matter how small. These celebrations reinforce positive behaviour and keep the momentum going.

In conclusion, accountability is not just about keeping you in line; it's about enriching your journey with support, guidance, and a sense of shared purpose. By consciously integrating accountability into your goal-setting process, you not only increase your chances of success but also make the journey more enjoyable and fulfilling.

6. Unrealistic Expectations: Setting Achievable Goals

"A goal should scare you a little, and excite you a lot." – Joe Vitale

In the quest to transform our lives, we often set our sights on the stars – ambitious, lofty goals that promise to usher in sweeping changes. While ambition is a powerful motivator, setting goals too high or too quickly can become a recipe for disappointment. It's like trying to leap to the top of a staircase in a single bound – both impractical and risky.

Imagine your goals as a mountain you wish to conquer. Setting goals that are too ambitious is like aiming to reach the summit in one day without proper preparation or acclimatisation. The result? Exhaustion, disappointment, and a decreased likelihood of trying again.

The secret to effective goal setting lies in balancing aspiration with attainability – setting goals that stretch your abilities yet remain within the realm of possibility.

Assess Your Starting Point: Take a realistic look at where you currently stand – your skills, resources, and constraints. Understanding your starting point helps in setting goals that are challenging yet achievable.

Embrace Incremental Progress: Instead of aiming for a drastic transformation overnight, focus on small, incremental changes. Like building a house brick by brick, small steps lead to substantial structures.

Define Clear, Measurable Goals: Vague goals breed vague results. Be specific about what you want to achieve and how you will measure progress.

Set Timeframes, But Be Flexible: While it's important to set deadlines, be prepared to adjust them if needed. Flexibility is not a sign of weakness, but of wisdom and resilience.

Seek Feedback and Advice: Sometimes, we're too close to our own goals to see them objectively. Seeking feedback from trusted mentors or peers can provide valuable perspective on the realism of our goals.

Celebrate Milestones: Acknowledge and celebrate each achievement, no matter how small. These celebrations reinforce your progress and motivate you to keep moving forward.

Learn from Setbacks: If a goal proves too ambitious, don't view it as a failure. Instead, analyse what you can learn from the experience and how you can adjust your approach.

Stay Adaptable: Life is unpredictable. Be ready to modify your goals as circumstances change. Adaptability is a key ingredient in the recipe for success.

In conclusion, setting realistic and achievable goals is a balancing act – one that involves aiming high enough to challenge yourself, but not so high that the goal becomes unattainable. By starting small, celebrating progress, and remaining adaptable, you lay down a sturdy foundation for achieving your dreams, one step at a time.

Motivation and Commitment: Keeping the Momentum Going

Fuelling Your Journey Towards Change

Staying motivated and committed can be challenging, especially when progress seems slow or obstacles arise. Here are some effective strategies to maintain motivation and commitment to your goals:

1. Remember Your 'Why'

> *"He who has a 'why' to live for can bear almost any how." –*
> *Friedrich Nietzsche*

At the heart of every goal lies a powerful motivator, a core reason that sparked the journey – your 'why.' In the pursuit of our ambitions, it's easy to get caught up in the hows and whats, losing sight of this fundamental driver. Reconnecting with your 'why' is like finding your compass in a storm; it can guide you back to motivation and clarity.

Imagine your 'why' as the beacon shining through the fog, guiding ships to safe harbour. When the waters of your journey become turbulent, when the waves of doubt and the winds of distraction buffet your sails, it's this beacon that guides you home.

Document Your Reasons: When you first set your goal, write down why it's important to you. This could be to improve your health, to grow as a person, or to achieve a sense of fulfilment. Keep this document somewhere you can see it regularly.

Visualise the Impact: Spend time visualising the positive impact achieving this goal will have on your life. Imagine the feelings of accomplishment, the improved quality of life, and the personal growth that will come.

Create Reminders: Set up daily reminders of your 'why.' This could be a note on your mirror, a background on your phone, or a daily alarm with a motivational quote.

Share Your Purpose: Talk about your goals and why they matter to you with friends, family, or a support group. Speaking your 'why' out loud reinforces its importance and can reignite your passion.

Reflect Regularly: Set aside time each week to reflect on your progress and reconnect with your 'why.' This can be through meditation, journaling, or simply quiet contemplation.

Align Actions with Purpose: Regularly assess whether your actions are aligned with your 'why.' If they're not, it might be time to adjust your approach.

Seek Inspiration: Read stories, listen to podcasts, or watch documentaries about people who achieved similar goals. Their journeys can rekindle your enthusiasm and commitment.

Embrace Flexibility: Sometimes, your 'why' can evolve. Be open to this evolution and adjust your goals accordingly.

In conclusion, your 'why' is not just the reason you start; it's the fuel that keeps you going. In moments of doubt or stagnation, revisiting your 'why' can reignite your motivation and renew your commitment to your journey. Remember, the strength of your commitment to your goal is directly related to the clarity and importance of your 'why.'

"The two most important days in your life are the day you are born and the day you find out why." – Mark Twain

[73]

2. Set Mini-Goals

"Success is the sum of small efforts, repeated day in and day out."
. *– Robert Collier*

In the pursuit of grand ambitions, it's easy to be daunted by the sheer scale of the challenge. The secret to climbing this mountain lies in the art of setting mini-goals – smaller, achievable targets that pave the path to your ultimate destination.

Imagine your main goal as a mountain peak shrouded in clouds – majestic, but seemingly unreachable. Mini-goals are the stepping stones that form a winding path up the mountain. Each step might not seem significant on its own, but together, they lead you to the summit.

Break It Down: Start by dissecting your main goal into smaller, more manageable parts. If your goal is to run a marathon, your mini-goals might include running a certain distance each week, gradually increasing your stamina, and participating in shorter races.

Set Clear Milestones: Define clear, measurable milestones for each mini-goal. These act as checkpoints to track your progress and keep you motivated.

Celebrate Small Victories: Acknowledge and celebrate each mini-goal you achieve. These celebrations reinforce your progress and motivate you to tackle the next step.

Focus on the Next Step: Instead of constantly looking at the summit, focus on the next step in front of you. This helps reduce overwhelm and keeps you grounded in the present.

Adjust as Needed: Be flexible with your mini-goals. If you find a particular step too challenging or too easy, adjust it to better suit your pace.

Visualise Each Step: Spend time visualising the completion of each mini-goal. This mental rehearsal prepares you for action and success.

Keep the End in Sight: While focusing on mini-goals, don't lose sight of your ultimate goal. Remind yourself how each step brings you closer to that grand vision.

Find Accountability: Share your mini-goals with someone who can hold you accountable. This could be a friend, a coach, or a support group.

In conclusion, mini-goals are the secret ingredients to achieving larger ambitions. They transform a daunting journey into a series of manageable steps, each one a victory in its own right. By setting, achieving, and celebrating these mini-goals, you create a rhythm of success that propels you toward your ultimate destination.

"The journey of a thousand miles begins with one step." – Lao Tzu

3. Visualise Success

"The only limits in our life are those we impose on ourselves." – Bob Proctor

In the quest to turn dreams into reality, one of the most potent tools at our disposal is the power of visualisation. It's a technique used by athletes, entrepreneurs, and achievers in various fields – a method of mentally rehearsing success.

Imagine your goal as a masterpiece yet to be painted. Each brushstroke of visualisation adds colour and detail to this picture, transforming it from a vague concept into a tangible reality. This mental imagery is not mere daydreaming; it's an active creation process.

Dedicate Time for Visualisation: Set aside a quiet time each day to visualise your success. Whether it's in the morning, during a break, or before you sleep, make this a consistent part of your routine.

Be Vivid and Detailed: When visualising, be as vivid and detailed as possible. If your goal is to give a successful presentation, imagine the room, the audience, the feeling of confidence, the sound of your voice, and the applause at the end.

Engage All Your Senses: Bring all your senses into this visualisation. What do you see, hear, feel, and even smell in this scene of success? The more senses involved, the more real it becomes.

Embrace the Emotions: Feel the emotions that come with achieving your goal. Joy, pride, relief, and gratitude – let these feelings wash over you during your visualisation.

Use Guided Imagery: If you find it hard to visualise on your own, consider guided imagery resources, like audio recordings or scripts, to help lead your imagination.

Create a Vision Board: Complement your mental visualisation with a physical one. A vision board with images and words representing your goal can reinforce your mental imagery.

Practice Regularly: Like any skill, visualisation gets better with practice. The more you do it, the more natural and effective it becomes.

Combine with Action: While visualisation is powerful, it needs to be combined with action. Use the motivation and clarity gained from your visualisation to fuel your real-world efforts.

In conclusion, visualisation is not just a tool for creating a vision of success; it's a way to prime your mind and body to make that vision a reality. By regularly painting the picture of your success in your mind, you gradually align your thoughts and actions with your goal, turning the intangible into the achievable.

"Visualise this thing that you want, see it, feel it, believe in it. Make your mental blue print, and begin to build." – Robert Collier

4. Create a Routine

"We are what we repeatedly do. Excellence, then, is not an act, but a habit." – Aristotle

In the symphony of goal achievement, consistency is the rhythm that drives the melody forward. Creating a routine, a set of habitual actions aligned with your goals, is like laying down a track for a train. Once the track is laid, the journey becomes smoother, and maintaining momentum becomes effortless.

Imagine your goal as a destination you're trying to reach. Without a map or a set path, the journey can be erratic and full of detours. A well-defined routine acts as a clear path towards your destination, ensuring each step you take moves you closer to your goal.

Identify Key Activities: Start by identifying activities that directly contribute to your goal. If your aim is to improve health, these might include exercise, meal planning, and meditation.

Craft a Daily Routine: Integrate these activities into your daily life. Set specific times for them, creating a structure that becomes your daily rhythm. Consistency is key – the more regular the activity, the more ingrained it becomes in your life.

Start Small: If establishing a new routine feels daunting, start small. Incorporate one or two activities and gradually build up. Remember, a journey of a thousand miles begins with a single step.

Plan for the Week Ahead: Each week, take a few minutes to plan how your goal-related activities will fit into your schedule. This helps in foreseeing and managing potential conflicts.

Create Rituals: Turn your activities into rituals. Rituals carry a sense of importance and help in mentally preparing you for the task. This could be as simple as a pre-workout stretch or a five-minute meditation before starting work.

Use Reminders and Alarms: In the early stages, use reminders or alarms to keep you on track. Over time, these activities will become second nature.

Adapt and Modify: Be flexible and willing to modify your routine as needed. If something isn't working, adjust it until it fits comfortably into your life.

Reflect and Adjust: Regularly reflect on your routine. Is it helping you progress towards your goal? What changes could make it more effective?

Reward Consistency: Celebrate your consistency. Each day you stick to your routine, you move one step closer to your goal.

In conclusion, building a routine is about creating a consistent pattern of behaviour that becomes almost automatic. This doesn't mean rigidity; it's about finding a rhythm that works for you and aligns with your goals. A well-crafted routine lays down the rails on which the train of your progress runs smoothly, taking you closer to your destination with each passing day.

"The secret of your future is hidden in your daily routine." – Mike Murdock

5. Find Support

"No man is an island, entire of itself; every man is a piece of the continent, a part of the main." – John Donne

In the journey of goal achievement, the path can sometimes be solitary and daunting. However, surrounding yourself with a supportive network transforms this solitary trek into a communal journey, filled with encouragement, accountability, and shared joy.

Imagine your goal as a seed you plant in the garden of your life. Like any seed, it requires the right environment to grow – sunlight, water, and nourishing soil. Your support system is like the sun and rain to your seed, providing the essential elements of motivation and encouragement needed for growth.

Choose Your Support Wisely: Surround yourself with people who believe in your goals and in you. This could be friends, family, mentors, or members of a support group.

Communicate Openly: Share your aspirations, the reasons behind them, and the challenges you face. Open communication fosters understanding and better support.

Celebrate Together: Celebrate your victories, no matter how small, with your support system. Let them share in your joy and success.

Seek Constructive Feedback: Encourage your support network to provide honest, constructive feedback. Sometimes, an outside perspective can offer valuable insights.

Offer Mutual Support: Support is a two-way street. Be there for your supporters in their endeavours, creating a mutually beneficial and nurturing environment.

Leverage Different Strengths: Different people offer different kinds of support. Some might be great at motivating you, while others might be better at offering practical help or advice.

Join or Create a Support Group: If you don't have an existing network, consider joining or creating a support group. This could be a physical group or an online community.

Acknowledge the Importance of Support: Recognise and appreciate the role of your support system in your journey. Gratitude strengthens relationships and builds a more robust support network.

Use Support to Stay Accountable: Regular check-ins with your support system can help keep you accountable and on track towards your goals.

In conclusion, a support system is not just a luxury; it's a crucial component of your journey towards achieving your goals. This network of encouragement and accountability acts as a catalyst, propelling you forward, uplifting you during lows, and celebrating with you during highs. Remember, the journey towards your dreams need not be a solitary one – with the strength of togetherness, every step becomes more meaningful and achievable.

"Alone we can do so little; together we can do so much." – Helen Keller

6. Reward Yourself

*"Don't wait until you've reached your goal to be proud of yourself. Be proud of every step you take toward reaching that goal." –
Unknown*

In the marathon of goal achievement, rewards are like the refreshment stations dotted along the route. They provide a moment of celebration, a burst of joy, and a tangible acknowledgement of your progress. Setting up a reward system for reaching certain milestones is not just about giving yourself a treat; it's a powerful psychological strategy to maintain motivation and enthusiasm.

Imagine each milestone on your journey as a checkpoint in a grand adventure. Each checkpoint reached is a cause for celebration, a moment to pause, reflect, and reward yourself for the distance covered.

Identify Meaningful Rewards: Choose rewards that are meaningful and desirable to you. This could be as simple as a favourite cup of coffee, a movie night, or something more significant like a weekend getaway.

Align Rewards with Goals: Ensure your rewards are in line with your overall goals. For instance, if your goal is weight loss, rewarding yourself with unhealthy food might be counterproductive. Instead, consider a spa day or new workout gear.

Set Clear Milestones: Define clear criteria for what constitutes reaching a milestone. This clarity removes ambiguity and makes the reward more satisfying.

Scale Your Rewards: Not all milestones are equal. Scale your rewards to match the significance of the milestone. Bigger achievements deserve bigger rewards.

Celebrate Small Wins: Don't just wait for the big victories. Celebrate the small wins too. These are the steps that build up to large successes.

Share Your Success: Sometimes, the best reward is sharing your success with others. Celebrate your milestones with friends, family, or your support group.

Keep a Reward Journal: Document your milestones and the rewards you've given yourself. This journal serves as a motivational record of your journey.

Use Rewards as Motivation: When facing a challenging task, remind yourself of the reward waiting at the end. This anticipation can be a powerful motivator.

Stay Flexible with Rewards: Be open to changing your rewards. What might seem appealing at the start of a journey might change as you progress.

In conclusion, rewarding yourself for reaching milestones isn't just about indulgence; it's a crucial strategy in maintaining motivation and momentum. It's a way of honouring your hard work, of acknowledging the effort and dedication you've put into your journey. These moments of celebration infuse joy into the process, making the pursuit of your goals not just an end in itself but a journey worth cherishing every step of the way.

"Remember to celebrate milestones as you prepare for the road ahead." – Nelson Mandela

7. Keep a Progress Journal

"The unexamined life is not worth living." – Socrates

In the odyssey of personal achievement and growth, keeping a progress journal is akin to charting a map of your journey. It serves not just as a record of where you've been, but also as a guide to where you're going. By documenting your journey, you create a tangible narrative of your progress, learning experiences, and the evolution of your strategies and goals.

Imagine your progress journal as a treasure map, where X marks not just the spot of your final goal, but also the milestones along the way. Each entry in your journal is a step on this map, marking the path you've taken, the obstacles you've navigated, and the discoveries you've made.

Start with Your Why: Begin your journal by documenting why you set your goals. This initial entry serves as a reminder of your core motivations.

Record Regular Entries: Make regular entries in your journal. This could be daily, weekly, or at any frequency that suits your journey. The key is consistency.

Celebrate Achievements: Note down every achievement, no matter how small. These entries are milestones that mark your progress.

Reflect on Challenges: Use your journal to reflect on challenges and setbacks. What lessons did they teach you? How did they shape your journey?

Track Patterns and Habits: Over time, your journal can reveal patterns and habits – both helpful and hindering. Use these insights to adjust your strategies.

Include Emotional Reflections: Document not just your actions, but also your emotions and thoughts. This holistic approach provides deeper insights into your journey.

Review and Adjust: Periodically review your journal. This review can offer valuable perspectives and show you how far you've come.

Use Visual Elements: If you're visually inclined, include drawings, charts, or photos in your journal. These elements can make the process more engaging and the journal more vivid.

Keep it Personal and Honest: Your progress journal is a personal document. Be honest and open in your entries. The more truthful you are, the more useful the journal is.

In conclusion, a progress journal is more than a record; it's a tool for reflection, motivation, and strategy. It's a chronicle of your growth, a mirror reflecting your journey, and a guide pointing towards future paths. By keeping a progress journal, you not only document your journey, but you also learn from it, gaining insights and wisdom that can be applied to future endeavours and life itself.

"Journal writing is a voyage to the interior." – Christina Baldwin

8. Stay Flexible

"Stay committed to your decisions, but stay flexible in your approach." – Tony Robbins

In the ever-evolving journey of goal achievement, rigidity can often be a hidden enemy. The world around us is in constant flux, and our paths to success are rarely straight or predictable. Flexibility in your goals and approach is like having a compass that adapts to the changing winds, helping you navigate through unforeseen challenges and altered circumstances.

Imagine your goals as a river flowing towards the ocean. While the destination is constant, the river's course may twist and turn, adapting to the landscape it traverses. In the same way, being open to adjusting your goals allows you to flow around obstacles, rather than crashing against them.

Reassess Regularly: Periodically step back to evaluate your goals and the path you're on. Is this path still viable, or do you need to carve a new one?

Embrace Change as Opportunity: View changes not as setbacks, but as opportunities for growth and learning. Each change is a chance to reassess and improve your approach.

Set Goals with Open Ends: When setting goals, leave room for adjustments. Rather than setting rigid timelines or overly specific outcomes, focus on the broader vision.

Develop a Problem-Solving Mind-Set: When faced with obstacles, instead of giving up, ask yourself, "How can I work through this?" This mind-set turns challenges into stepping stones.

Seek Multiple Pathways: For every goal, consider multiple pathways to achieve it. This approach means if one path is blocked, you have alternatives to explore.

Listen to Feedback: Be open to feedback from mentors, peers, or even your own experiences. Feedback is a valuable source of information for making necessary adjustments.

Balance Consistency with Flexibility: While consistency in action is key, it should be balanced with the flexibility to adapt those actions as needed.

Mind-set of Experimentation: Treat your goal achievement process as an experiment. Some things will work, and others won't. The key is to learn and adapt.

Practice Self-Compassion: Be kind to yourself when changes occur. Flexibility often requires letting go of old plans and forgiving oneself for any missteps along the way.

In conclusion, staying flexible in the pursuit of your goals is a testament to your commitment and resilience. It's about making the most of the journey, learning from the detours, and continually moving towards your destination, even if the path there looks different than you originally planned. In a world that is constantly changing, adaptability is not just a skill; it's a necessity.

"The measure of intelligence is the ability to change." – Albert Einstein

9. Practice Self-Compassion

"The most terrifying thing is to accept oneself completely." – Carl Jung

In the intricate dance of goal setting and achievement, we often become our own harshest critics. We push ourselves relentlessly, and when faced with setbacks, we are quick to judge and condemn our efforts. This section is an invitation to shift that perspective, to practice self-compassion, and recognise that the path to our goals is often winding and fraught with challenges.

Imagine your journey toward your goals as a garden you are tending. Each goal is a plant in this garden. Just as plants need sunlight, water, and care to grow, your goals need effort, time, and a nurturing touch of self-compassion.

Acknowledge Your Humanity: Recognise that being human means being flawed and imperfect. Embrace your humanity with all its imperfections and vulnerabilities.

Reframe Setbacks as Learning Opportunities: Instead of viewing setbacks as failures, see them as opportunities to learn and grow. Every setback teaches you something valuable.

Speak to Yourself Kindly: Pay attention to your self-talk. Replace critical or negative thoughts with kinder, more supportive messages.

Celebrate Your Efforts: Acknowledge the effort you put in, regardless of the outcome. Effort is a success in itself.

Allow Yourself to Feel: Give yourself permission to feel disappointed, sad, or frustrated, but don't dwell there. Allow these emotions to be expressed and then gently guide yourself back to a place of motivation and action.

Practice Mindfulness: Engage in mindfulness practices. Mindfulness helps you to stay present and reduces the tendency to ruminate on past "failures" or worry excessively about the future.

Seek Support: When being kind to yourself is difficult, turn to friends, family, or mentors who can offer a compassionate perspective.

Remember Your Progress: Keep a journal or a list of achievements, no matter how small. Remind yourself of how far you've come whenever you feel down.

Self-Care Rituals: Engage in regular self-care rituals. This could be anything from a relaxing bath, a walk in nature, or simply some quiet time with a book.

In conclusion, practicing self-compassion is not about making excuses for not meeting goals. It's about treating yourself with the same kindness and understanding you would offer to a good friend in a similar situation. It's about recognising that the path to success is often non-linear and that setbacks are not only inevitable but also invaluable parts of the learning process. In the end, how you journey through your path is as important as reaching the destination itself.

"Talk to yourself like you would to someone you love." – Brené Brown

Chapter 8: Strategies for Overcoming Depression
Daily Routines and Habits: Foundations for Mental Well-Being

Crafting a Routine That Nurtures Your Mind

In the journey towards better mental health, establishing a daily routine and healthy habits can be transformative. Consistent routines and habits provide structure, reduce stress, and promote a sense of stability and control.

1. Morning Rituals: Starting Your Day Right

"Each morning we are born again. What we do today is what matters most." – Buddha

The way we usher in each new day sets the tempo for our entire journey through its hours. Morning rituals are not just actions; they are the sacred tuning of our life's instrument, preparing us for the symphony of the day ahead. These rituals are the foundation stones upon which we build a day of purpose, positivity, and productivity.

Imagine the first light of dawn as the opening notes of a grand symphony. How you choose to start your day is like choosing the melody that will play throughout your day. A morning ritual is your personal overture, a deliberate and harmonious sequence that sets the tone for what follows.

Mindful Breathing: Begin each day with the simple yet profound practice of mindful breathing. Dedicate a few quiet minutes after waking to breathe deeply and consciously. Feel each breath as it fills your lungs, grounds your thoughts, and centres your spirit. This practice is the opening note, setting a calm and focused tone.

Gratitude Journaling: Embrace the power of gratitude by keeping a journal. Each morning, write down three things you are thankful for. This could be as simple as a sunny day, a loving pet, or the comfort of your home. Gratitude tunes your mind to positivity, transforming your outlook and opening your heart to the day's blessings.

Physical Awakening: Introduce some form of physical activity into your morning. Whether it's gentle stretching, a yoga flow, or a brisk walk in the fresh air, engage your body in a way that resonates with you. This movement is like a crescendo in your morning symphony, energising your body and elevating your mood.

Nourish Your Body: Pay attention to your morning nourishment. A healthy breakfast, rich in nutrients and care, fuels your body and respects its needs. This is not just eating; it's an act of self-love.

Set Your Intentions: Take a moment to set your intentions for the day. What do you wish to accomplish? How do you want to feel? What impact do you want to have? These intentions are your day's melody, guiding your actions and thoughts.

Embrace Positivity: Conclude your morning ritual with a positive affirmation or a motivational quote. Let these words be the harmonious closing chords of your morning routine, sending you into your day with a sense of purpose and optimism.

In conclusion, by embracing these morning rituals, you create a daily routine that not only nourishes your mind and body but also aligns your spirit with a mind-set of positivity and productivity. Each day is a new opportunity, a blank canvas upon which you can paint the life you desire. Let your morning rituals be the brushstrokes that start this beautiful creation.

2. Structured Work Time: Managing Stress and Productivity

"The key is in not spending time, but in investing it." – Stephen R. Covey

In the grand orchestra of life, where various melodies of personal and professional responsibilities intertwine, orchestrating your work time effectively becomes paramount in crafting a symphony of balance and productivity. This section focuses on transforming your daily work schedule into a well-composed masterpiece, harmonising productivity with well-being, and keeping the discordant notes of stress at bay.

Visualise your daily work schedule as a musical score, where each note represents a task, and the rests symbolise breaks. Just as a well-composed piece of music has a balance of notes and rests, your workday should have a harmonious arrangement of focused work and rejuvenating pauses.

Prioritise with Purpose: Begin each day by identifying and prioritising your tasks. Tackle the most significant and challenging tasks first, when your mental symphony is fresh and vibrant. This prioritisation is akin to playing the key notes of your day's melody.

Compose with Breaks: Integrate regular, intentional breaks into your schedule. These are the rests in your day's score. Just as music requires pauses to enhance its beauty, your mind needs these gaps to prevent burnout and rejuvenate. These breaks could be a short walk, a meditation session, or simply a moment of quiet.

Set Boundaries with Harmony: Establish clear boundaries between your work and personal life. Define specific working hours and respect them as you would a sacred rhythm. This separation ensures that the professional tempo doesn't overwhelm the personal, allowing you to be fully present in both realms.

Embrace a Flexible Tempo: While structure is important, so is flexibility. Be willing to adjust your schedule if unexpected tasks arise. Flexibility in your routine is like an improvisational element in music, adding richness and adaptability to your day.

Cultivate a Mindful Workspace: Create a workspace that encourages focus and calm. This could involve organising your physical space, minimising distractions, or incorporating elements that bring you peace, such as plants or calming background music.

Reflect and Adjust: At the end of each day, take a moment to reflect on your schedule. What worked well? What could be improved? This reflection is your daily review of the day's composition, allowing you to fine-tune your approach for future days.

In conclusion, by adopting a structured yet adaptable approach to managing your work or study time, you compose a daily rhythm that fosters productivity and mitigates stress. This careful orchestration of your tasks, breaks, and boundaries sets the stage for not just a successful day, but a balanced and fulfilling life. Let each day be a harmonious blend of focus and relaxation, a symphony that resonates with the rhythms of efficiency and well-being.

3. Mindful Eating: Nourishing Your Body and Mind

"One cannot think well, love well, and sleep well, if one has not dined well." – Virginia Woolf

In the intricate dance of maintaining holistic well-being, the act of eating transforms from a mere routine to an art form – a symphony where every bite resonates with the rhythm of health and mindfulness. This section explores the profound impact of mindful eating, not just as a means of physical nourishment but as a celebration of food that nurtures both body and soul.

Visualise your daily meals as a grand orchestra, where each ingredient plays a vital role, each flavour contributes to the harmony, and the act of eating is the conductor, bringing it all together in a beautiful melody of health and awareness.

Select the Finest Ingredients: Begin your journey with thoughtful food choices. Opt for foods that are rich in nutrients, vitamins, and minerals. These are the notes that compose the melody of your meal – fresh vegetables, fruits, whole grains, lean proteins, and healthy fats. Each ingredient should support not just your physical well-being but also your mental clarity and emotional balance.

The Ritual of Preparation: View the preparation of your food as a sacred ritual. The act of chopping, cooking, and arranging your food is an opportunity to connect with the process of nurturing yourself.

The Art of Mindful Consumption: As you eat, be fully present. Engage all your senses. Notice the colours, the textures, and the aromas. Taste each bite with attention and appreciation. This mindfulness slows down the eating process, enhances digestion, and brings a deeper sense of satisfaction.

Listen to Your Body's Symphony: Tune into your body's cues. Eat when you're hungry and stop when you're comfortably full. Learn to differentiate physical hunger from emotional hunger.

Savour Each Note: Slow down and savour each mouthful. This not only allows for better digestion but also lets you truly appreciate the food and the effort that went into preparing it.

Nourish Beyond the Plate: Understand that mindful eating is not just about the food on your plate. It's about the environment, the company, and the mind-set with which you eat. Create a peaceful eating environment, free from distractions like TV or smartphones.

Reflect and Adjust: After each meal, take a moment to reflect on how it made you feel. Did it bring satisfaction and energy? Or discomfort and lethargy? Use these reflections to fine-tune your food choices and eating habits.

In conclusion, by embracing the principles of mindful eating, you transform your meals into a holistic experience that nourishes every part of your being. Each meal becomes a moment of connection with your body, a celebration of nourishment, and a step towards a healthier, more balanced self.

4. Evening Wind-Down: Preparing for Restful Sleep

"Sleep is the best meditation." – Dalai Lama

As the sun sets and the day's hustle fades into the twilight, the way we bid farewell to our waking hours plays a crucial role in our journey towards restful sleep. An evening wind-down routine is not just a series of actions; it's a sacred ritual, a gentle serenade that lulls your body and mind into a state of peaceful slumber.

Envision your evening routine as a soothing sonata, a musical composition that gradually softens, slowing the tempo of your day and transitioning you into the calming embrace of the night.

Embrace the Digital Sunset: Begin your evening ritual with a digital detox. As the sun sets, let your screens go dark too. This break from digital devices helps to reduce mental stimulation and signals to your brain that the day is drawing to a close. The absence of blue light from screens also aids in the natural production of melatonin, the sleep hormone.

Serenade with Relaxation: Introduce calming activities into your evening. This could be immersing yourself in the pages of a good book, soaking in a warm, aromatic bath, or flowing through a sequence of gentle yoga poses. These activities release the physical and mental tensions of the day, tuning your body and mind to a restful frequency.

Reflective Journaling: Set aside time for reflective journaling. Write about the day's experiences, your feelings, or plan for the morrow. This act of putting thoughts to paper is a therapeutic release, clearing your mind of clutter and quieting the inner chatter that can disturb sleep.

Create a Sleep-Inducing Environment: Prepare your sleeping area to be a tranquil haven. Dim the lights, perhaps light a candle with a soothing scent, and ensure your bedding is comfortable and inviting. This environment sets the stage for your sleep sonata.

Mindful Meditation: Consider ending your day with a mindfulness meditation or a guided sleep visualisation. These practices help in cantering your thoughts and grounding your emotions, preparing you for deep, restorative sleep.

Consistency is Key: Make your evening ritual a consistent practice. Just as a familiar lullaby can signal a child's mind to prepare for sleep, a regular routine cues your body and mind to unwind and relax.

In conclusion, by integrating these practices into your evening routine, you craft a cocoon of calm, setting the stage for a night of deep, restorative sleep. This nightly ritual becomes a cherished symphony of serenity, a lullaby for the soul, preparing you for the rejuvenation that only a peaceful slumber can provide.

5. Consistency is Key

"Small disciplines repeated with consistency every day lead to great achievements gained slowly over time." – John C. Maxwell

In the grand tapestry of life, where each thread represents a day, the power of consistency emerges as the weaver's hand, guiding the formation of patterns that define the fabric of our existence. This section explores the transformative power of consistency in establishing routines, emphasising that regular practice isn't just about discipline; it's about creating a symphony of habits that resonate harmoniously with our life's goals.

Imagine your daily routine as threads in a tapestry. Each thread on its own may seem insignificant, but when woven consistently, day after day, they form a beautiful and complex design. The key to this beautiful formation is consistency – the regular, rhythmic repetition that creates lasting habits.

Start with Small Threads: Begin by integrating small, manageable habits into your daily routine. It's easier to maintain consistency with small actions than with large, overwhelming changes.

Stitch Day by Day: Focus on being consistent day by day. Don't worry about the long term. Concentrate on weaving the thread of today.

Create Trigger Points: Establish specific cues or triggers for your habits. For instance, meditating right after brushing your teeth in the morning. These triggers become signals that initiate your routine.

Celebrate the Stitches: Acknowledge and celebrate each day you maintain your routine. These small celebrations reinforce your commitment and make the process enjoyable.

Maintain a Habit Tracker: Consider keeping a habit tracker. This can be a simple calendar where you mark off each day you complete your routine. Visually seeing your progress can be incredibly motivating.

Embrace the Rhythm of Regularity: Find joy in the regularity of your routines. Just as a dancer finds joy in the rhythm of their steps, find satisfaction in the rhythm of your daily practices.

Be Patient with the Tapestry: Understand that the beauty of the tapestry takes time to emerge. Be patient with yourself and trust that the consistent weaving of your habits will create something beautiful in your life.

Adjust the Patterns: If a routine isn't serving you, be willing to adjust it. Consistency doesn't mean inflexibility. It's about maintaining the rhythm, not about sticking to a routine that doesn't work.

In conclusion, by embracing the principle of consistency, you transform your routines into natural and integral parts of your daily life. You move from consciously cultivating habits to unconsciously living them. These habits then weave the rich tapestry of your life, each consistent thread adding to the strength and beauty of the whole.

Cognitive and Behavioural Techniques: Reshaping Your Mind-set

Harnessing the Power of Thought and Action

Cognitive and behavioural techniques are powerful tools for changing the way we think and act. These techniques are essential for overcoming mental health challenges like depression, anxiety, and stress.

1. Cognitive Restructuring: Rewiring Your Thoughts

"The mind is everything; what you think, you become." – Buddha

Embark on the transformative journey of cognitive restructuring, a mental alchemy that reshapes and rewires the landscape of your thoughts. This journey is not just about changing what you think; it's about changing how you think. It's a voyage towards a mind-set that is balanced, rational, and resilient.

Imagine your thought process as a garden. Over time, weeds of negative and irrational thoughts may have grown, entangling themselves around the flowers of your mind. Cognitive restructuring is the process of tending this garden – removing the weeds and nurturing the flowers.

Unearthing Hidden Thoughts: The first step is to become a vigilant gardener, identifying the weeds – the automatic negative thoughts that often go unnoticed but deeply influence your emotions and behaviours. This book will guide you in recognising these hidden thought patterns, bringing them into the light of awareness.

Analysing the Roots: Once these thoughts are uncovered, we delve into critically analysing and challenging them. It's about questioning their truth, understanding their origins, and assessing their impact. This process is like examining the roots of the weeds, understanding how they've grown and spread.

Planting Seeds of Rationality: The final step is replacing the old, unhelpful thoughts with new, balanced ones. This isn't about planting flowers of extreme positivity but cultivating seeds of realism and rationality. It's finding that fertile ground where thoughts are realistic, balanced, and constructive.

Practice Mindful Awareness: Develop the habit of mindfulness, being present and aware of your thoughts without judgment. This awareness is the first step in recognising negative thought patterns.

Embrace Curiosity: Approach your thoughts with curiosity rather than criticism. Ask yourself, "Why do I think this way? Is there another way to see this situation?"

Use Thought Records: Keep a thought record – a journal where you write down negative thoughts, their triggers, and the emotions they evoke. Then, work on reframing these thoughts in a more balanced way.

Seek the Grey Areas: Life is rarely black and white. Train your mind to see the grey areas, the nuances in situations, rather than jumping to conclusions.

Affirm Rational Beliefs: Regularly affirm and reinforce rational beliefs. This could be through daily affirmations, meditation, or cognitive exercises.

Consult a Guide: Sometimes, the journey of cognitive restructuring can benefit from a guide. A therapist or counsellor can provide valuable insights and tools in navigating this process.

By undertaking the journey of cognitive restructuring, you transform your internal landscape. You learn to cultivate a garden of thoughts that are grounded in reality, nurtured by rationality, and resilient to the storms of life. This mental transformation paves the way for emotional well-being and a more fulfilling life experience.

2. Mindfulness: Living in the Present Moment

"The present moment is filled with joy and happiness. If you are attentive, you will see it." – Thich Nhat Hanh

In the tapestry of life, each moment is a unique thread, vibrant and fleeting. Mindfulness is the art of weaving these threads with attention and intention, creating a tapestry that is rich in detail and deeply connected to the present. This section is an invitation to immerse yourself in the 'here and now', to embrace each moment with clarity and peace.

Imagine yourself as a boat in the vast ocean of time. Mindfulness is the anchor that grounds you in the present, preventing you from drifting aimlessly in the currents of past regrets or future anxieties.

Focused Breathing: Begin your journey into mindfulness with focused breathing. This technique is your anchor. Concentrate on each inhalation and exhalation – the way the air feels entering your nostrils, filling your lungs, and leaving your body. This simple act centres your mind and brings you back to the now.

Mindful Observation: Engage in the practice of mindful observation. This could be as simple as noticing the play of light on a surface, the texture of an object, or the sounds around you. Use all your senses to fully experience and connect with these details. This practice enriches your present experience, filling it with depth and awareness.

Embrace Mindful Activities: Integrate mindfulness into everyday activities. Whether you are eating, walking, or even doing household chores, do it with full awareness. Notice the colours, the tastes, the movements. Be completely immersed in the activity.

Non-judgmental Acceptance: Approach your thoughts and feelings with acceptance and without judgment. Acknowledge them as they are, without trying to suppress or change them. This acceptance creates a space of peace and clarity.

Cultivate a Mindful Environment: Create an environment that supports mindfulness. This could be a small corner in your home for meditation, a garden where you can connect with nature, or any space that encourages peaceful reflection.

Regular Practice: Like any skill, mindfulness grows stronger with regular practice. Dedicate a few minutes each day to mindfulness exercises. Over time, this practice will become a natural part of your daily life.

Mindful Reminders: Set reminders throughout your day to pause and practice mindfulness. It could be a note, an alarm, or a specific routine that prompts you to take a mindful moment.

By embracing mindfulness, you learn to live fully in each moment, to experience life in its entirety and richness. It is a journey of discovering the beauty and serenity that exists in the now, a path that leads to mental clarity and inner peace.

3. Behavioural Activation: Taking Action Against Depression

"Action is the foundational key to all success." – Pablo Picasso

In the shadowy valleys of depression, where motivation dims and joy seems a distant memory, the technique of behavioural activation emerges as a beacon of hope. This strategy is not just about doing; it's about engaging with life in a way that sparks a rekindling of enjoyment and fulfilment. It's a proactive dance against the inertia of depression, a step-by-step approach to reclaim your life's rhythm.

Visualise your journey through depression as walking through a dense, foggy forest. Behavioural activation is like finding a path lined with lanterns, each light representing an action that brings a moment of brightness and clarity.

Scheduling Pleasant Activities: Start by identifying activities that once brought you joy or new activities you'd like to explore. These could range from hobbies, social interactions, to simple pleasures like reading or walking in nature. Schedule these activities into your week, treating them as important appointments with yourself. These planned moments of joy act as beacons, illuminating your path through the fog.

Breaking Down Overwhelming Tasks: Look at the tasks or goals that feel overwhelming and break them down into smaller, manageable steps. Each step should be achievable and clear. This approach is like creating a series of stepping stones that gradually lead you out of the fog, one step at a time.

Creating a Reward System: Pair your tasks and activities with rewards. These rewards, no matter how small, serve as positive reinforcements, encouraging you to continue your journey of action.

Embracing a Routine of Engagement: Establish a daily routine that includes these activities and tasks. A routine creates a structure that can be incredibly helpful in combating the aimlessness and lack of motivation often experienced in depression.

Mindful Acknowledgement: As you engage in each activity, practice mindfulness. Be present in the moment, fully experiencing the activity. This presence can heighten the enjoyment and satisfaction derived from the action.

Reflect and Adjust: Regularly reflect on the activities and their impact on your mood. What worked well? What didn't? Use these insights to adjust your plan, adding more of what brings positivity and removing or altering what doesn't.

Seeking Support: Remember, you don't have to walk this path alone. Share your plan with a trusted friend, family member, or therapist who can offer support and encouragement.

By embracing the principles of behavioural activation, you re-engage with life in a way that brings light to the darkness of depression. Each action, each scheduled activity is a step towards reclaiming the joy and vibrancy of life. It's a journey of rediscovering the beauty that life has to offer, one small, deliberate step at a time.

4. Exposure Therapy: Facing Fears in a Controlled Way

"Courage is not the absence of fear, but the triumph over it." – *Nelson Mandela*

In the labyrinth of anxiety disorders, where fears cast long shadows and dictate the paths we take, exposure therapy emerges as a beacon of courage and transformation. This method is not merely about facing fears; it's a carefully charted journey towards reclaiming control, a process of gradually diminishing the power that fear has over your life.

Imagine your fear as a dark, mysterious forest that you've always avoided. Exposure therapy is like gradually venturing into this forest, first stepping into its edges and slowly going deeper, guided by the light of knowledge and the compass of professional support.

Understanding the Map of Exposure: Begin by understanding what exposure therapy entails. It's a journey of gradual and controlled confrontation with your fears, not a reckless plunge into the depths of terror. This understanding is your map, guiding you through the therapy.

Identifying the Fears: The first step is to clearly identify your fears. What specific situations or objects trigger your anxiety?

Recognising and naming these fears is like marking them on your map.

Creating a Hierarchy of Fears: Develop a hierarchy or a ladder of fears, starting from the least anxiety-inducing to the most. This hierarchy will guide your journey, ensuring that the exposure is gradual and manageable.

Taking the First Steps: Begin with the least threatening situation on your hierarchy. This controlled exposure can be real or imagined, depending on your therapy plan. These first steps are crucial; they're your initial forays into the forest of fear.

Incorporating Relaxation Techniques: Learn and practice relaxation techniques. These techniques are your tools to maintain calmness and control during exposure. They could be deep breathing, mindfulness, or grounding exercises.

Gradual Advancement: Slowly, as your comfort level increases, move up the hierarchy. With each step, the fear loses some of its power, the forest becomes less daunting.

Consistent Practice: Regular and consistent exposure is key. Each venture into the feared situation builds your confidence and reduces the fear response.

Reflect and Reassess: After each exposure session, reflect on the experience. What did you learn? How did it feel? This reflection is crucial for understanding and reinforcing your progress.

Professional Guidance: Exposure therapy is best navigated with the guidance of a therapist. Their expertise is like a guiding light, helping you find your way and adjust the therapy as needed.

Through the courageous journey of exposure therapy, you learn that the power of fear diminishes under the light of direct confrontation. It's a path that requires bravery, but with each step, you reclaim a piece of yourself that fear had taken. This journey is about transforming your relationship with fear, from one of avoidance to one of understanding and control.

5. Positive Reinforcement: Rewarding Positive Behaviours

"Your positive action combined with positive thinking results in success." – Shiv Khera

In the intricate dance of personal growth and self-improvement, the music of positive reinforcement and the harmony of positive language play pivotal roles. This section unveils how rewarding positive behaviours and reshaping our language can orchestrate a transformative impact on our lives, leading us towards success and well-being.

Imagine your journey towards your goals as a series of musical notes, each note representing a step or action. Positive reinforcement is the melody that makes these notes resonate, turning actions into habits.

Celebrating Small Victories: Begin by identifying and rewarding yourself for each small step towards your goal. These rewards could be as simple as a favourite treat, a relaxing bath, or time spent on a hobby. Each reward is a note of encouragement, reinforcing the behaviour that led to it.

Cultivating a Reward System: Create a system where positive actions are consistently acknowledged and rewarded. This system acts as a rhythm, guiding and motivating you to repeat these behaviours.

Acknowledge Your Progress: Regularly take time to reflect on and celebrate your progress. Acknowledging how far you've come plays a significant role in maintaining your motivation and commitment.

Recognising Negative Statements: The first step in transforming your language is to become aware of negative statements or thoughts. These are often hidden in everyday language, subtly influencing your mind-set and emotions.

Positive Reframing: Transform these negative statements into positive affirmations. Focus on what you wish to achieve, framing your language in a way that reflects your goals and aspirations.

The Power of Positive Affirmations: Create positive affirmations that resonate with your goals and repeat them daily. These affirmations are like a chorus, reinforcing your positive mind-set and helping you overcome challenges.

Embracing a Positive Vocabulary: Consciously choose words that are positive and empowering. Language shapes perception, and by changing your words, you can change your outlook.

Mindful Communication: Practice mindful communication with others. Use language that uplifts and encourages, creating a positive ripple effect in your interactions.

By integrating the principles of positive reinforcement and the power of positive language into your life, you compose a symphony of positivity. This symphony not only guides your actions and behaviours but also shapes your thoughts and perceptions, leading to a more fulfilling and successful life. Each note of positive reinforcement and each chord of positive language contributes to a harmonious melody that echoes throughout your journey.

Chapter 9: Strategies for Overcoming Anxiety
Cognitive Strategies: Reshaping Anxious Thoughts

Tackling Anxiety with the Mind's Power

Anxiety often stems from the way we think about and interpret situations. Cognitive strategies focus on identifying, challenging, and reframing anxious thoughts to reduce anxiety's impact.

1. Identifying Anxious Thoughts

When managing anxiety, the first and perhaps most crucial step is to become an adept observer of your own mind. This chapter is dedicated to developing the skill of recognising and labelling anxious thoughts, a key strategy in cognitive techniques for managing anxiety. It's about learning to distinguish the whispers of anxiety from the chorus of your everyday thoughts.

Visualise your mind as a vast, bustling city. Thoughts are like the myriad of people who walk its streets. Among them walk the shadowy figures of anxiety – elusive, often blending into the crowd. Identifying these figures is the first step in reclaiming the streets of your mind.

Awareness Training: Begin with training yourself to be an observer of your thoughts. This awareness is like learning to navigate the city. Pay attention to the thoughts that pass through your mind, especially during moments of discomfort or stress.

Recognising the Signs of Anxious Thoughts: Learn to recognise the hallmarks of anxious thoughts. They often involve worry about the future, rumination over the past, catastrophic thinking, or black-and-white perspectives.

Labelling the Thoughts: When you catch an anxious thought, label it. This act of labelling is akin to putting a pin on a map – it helps you to see the thought for what it is. You might say to yourself, "This is an anxiety thought."

Journaling the Journey: Keep a thought journal. Write down the anxious thoughts as you identify them. This journal becomes a map of your mind, helping you to recognise patterns and frequent areas where anxiety lurks.

Mindfulness as a Tool: Incorporate mindfulness practices. Mindfulness helps in grounding your thoughts to the present and observing your mental processes without judgment.

Cultivating Curiosity: Approach your thoughts with curiosity rather than fear or frustration. Ask yourself, "Why might I be feeling this way?" Understanding the root of your anxiety helps in addressing it more effectively.

Seeking Guidance on the Path: If identifying anxious thoughts becomes overwhelming, consider seeking guidance from a therapist. They can provide tools and techniques to enhance your self-awareness.

By mastering the art of identifying your anxious thoughts, you lay the foundation for cognitive strategies to manage anxiety. This skill allows you to navigate the city of your mind more effectively, recognising and reducing the power of the shadowy figures of anxiety. It's a journey of self-discovery, where you learn to understand and manage the complex landscape of your thoughts.

2. Challenging Anxious Thoughts

In the journey of managing anxiety, identifying anxious thoughts is akin to mapping the territory. The next crucial step is to question and challenge these thoughts, a mental art that disarms their power and reveals the reality behind the distortions. This section delves into the strategic questioning of your anxious thoughts, turning the lens of scrutiny onto the shadows they cast in your mind.

Imagine each anxious thought as a dubious character in the story of your mind. Challenging these characters involves engaging them in a dialogue, questioning their motives, and unveiling their inconsistencies.

Seeking Evidence: When an anxious thought arises, ask yourself, "Is there evidence that supports this thought?" This question is like shining a light on a shadow, seeking substance. Often, you'll find that the thought is more conjecture than reality.

Avoiding Mind-Traps: Question whether you are jumping to negative conclusions. Anxious thoughts often involve catastrophic or black-and-white thinking. Ask yourself, "Am I assuming the worst? Is there a more balanced way to view this situation?"

Exploring Alternatives: Consider alternative explanations or outcomes. Anxious thoughts tend to narrow your vision, focusing only on negative possibilities. By deliberately considering other outcomes, you widen your perspective, reducing the hold of anxiety.

Reality-Check: Remind yourself of past experiences. "Have I felt this way before, and were my fears realised?" Often, you'll find that past anxieties have been unfounded, which can help in mitigating current ones.

Consulting a Trusted Advisor: Sometimes, it's helpful to talk through your thoughts with someone you trust. A different perspective can provide a reality check and challenge the anxious thought more effectively.

Writing as a Tool of Inquiry: Journaling can be a powerful tool in challenging anxious thoughts. Write down the thought, then write down evidence against it, alternative viewpoints, and more balanced perspectives.

Practicing Regularly: Like any skill, challenging anxious thoughts gets easier with practice. Make it a regular mental exercise, and over time, you'll find it becomes a natural response to anxiety.

By mastering the art of challenging your anxious thoughts, you disarm their power over your emotions and behaviours. This process of cognitive cross-examination transforms the way you interact with your thoughts, leading to greater mental clarity and resilience. It's a journey of turning anxiety from a formidable foe into an understood and managed aspect of your mental landscape.

3. Reframing Thoughts

In the vast gallery of our minds, where thoughts are like paintings reflecting our perceptions of the world, the technique of reframing becomes an essential skill. This section explores the art of reframing – changing the canvas and perspective of your thoughts to paint a picture that's more positive, realistic, and empowering.

Imagine each of your thoughts as a brushstroke on a canvas. Some strokes create scenes of worry and doubt, while others paint confidence and hope. Reframing is like adjusting these strokes, changing a foreboding storm into a refreshing rain, or a barrier into a stepping stone.

Identify the Original Frame: The first step is to recognise the existing frame of your thoughts. What is the current narrative? For instance, a thought like, "This will be a disaster," frames the situation in a negative and hopeless light.

Understanding the Power of Perception: Acknowledge that the way you frame your thoughts significantly influences your emotions and actions. It's not just the situation, but your interpretation of it that shapes your experience.

Choosing a New Frame: Deliberately choose a new, more empowering frame for your thought. For example, shifting from "This will be a disaster" to "I'm nervous, but I have handled similar situations before," changes the narrative from one of despair to one of capability and hope.

[106]

Using Positive Language: Pay attention to the language you use. Words have power. Using positive and proactive language helps in reinforcing the new frame.

Reflect on Past Successes: Draw on past experiences where you've successfully navigated challenges. Reminding yourself of these can bolster your confidence and support the new frame.

Seek Alternative Views: Sometimes, seeing things from a different angle can be enlightening. Ask yourself, "How would someone I admire view this situation?"

Practice Regularly: Like any art, the skill of reframing takes practice. Make it a habit to identify and adjust the frames of your thoughts regularly.

Embracing Flexibility in Thought: Be open to the idea that there are multiple ways to view a situation. Flexibility in thinking allows for a broader and more adaptable perspective.

Through the art of reframing, you learn to repaint the scenes of your mind, transforming perspectives that hold you back into ones that empower and motivate you. This cognitive restructuring is not about denying reality but about choosing to see and experience it in a way that serves you better. It's about becoming the artist of your mental landscape, creating a masterpiece of perspective that reflects resilience, optimism, and realism.

Lifestyle Changes: Creating a Healthy Foundation for Mental Wellness

Managing anxiety isn't just about addressing thoughts and emotions; it also involves nurturing your body through healthy lifestyle choices. This section explores how diet, exercise, and sleep can profoundly impact anxiety levels.

1. Diet: Nourishing Your Body and Mind

"Let food be thy medicine and medicine be thy food." –
Hippocrates

In the delicate balance of mental and physical well-being, the role of diet plays a symphonic part, orchestrating a harmony that resonates through every aspect of our health. This section invites you on a journey to understand and embrace the profound impact of nutrition on mood and anxiety. It's about transforming our approach to eating, from mere sustenance to a mindful practice that nourishes both body and mind.

Imagine your diet as a beautifully composed melody, where each ingredient contributes to the overall harmony of your health. Just as a symphony is composed of different notes and rhythms, your diet should be a diverse blend of nutrients working in concert.

Embrace Whole Foods: Begin by incorporating whole foods into your diet. These are the natural, unprocessed notes in your nutritional symphony – whole grains, lean proteins, a colourful array of fruits and vegetables, and healthy fats. Each group plays its part in stabilising mood and energy.

Moderating the Extremes: Be mindful of sugar and caffeine, the loud and jarring notes that can disturb the harmony. High sugar intake and excessive caffeine can lead to crashes and exacerbate symptoms of anxiety. Moderation is key – it's about turning these elements from cacophony to harmony.

The Fluidity of Hydration: Like the gentle flow of a river, hydration is crucial for maintaining the balance. Dehydration can be a silent disruptor of mood and cognitive function. Ensure you drink enough water throughout the day, keeping the rhythm of your health flowing smoothly.

Mindful Eating: Pay attention to how foods make you feel. This isn't just about taste – it's about noticing the effects of different foods on your mood and energy levels. Mindful eating turns each meal into a moment of connection with your body, understanding its needs and reactions.

Listening to Your Body's Symphony: Tune into your body's signals. It will often tell you what it needs, whether it's more of certain nutrients or less of others. Learning to listen and respond to these signals is like fine-tuning an instrument.

Experiment and Adjust: Be open to experimenting with your diet and adjusting based on how you feel. Nutrition is not one-size-fits-all; it's a personal composition that you have the power to modify.

Seeking Harmonious Guidance: If you find it challenging to create a balanced diet, consider seeking advice from a nutritionist. They can help you compose a dietary plan that resonates with your individual health needs.

By embracing these principles, you transform your diet into a harmonious blend of nutrients that support not just your physical health but also your mental well-being. Each meal becomes an opportunity to nourish your body and soothe your mind, contributing to a symphony of overall health and harmony.

2. Exercise: The Natural Anxiety Reliever

"Exercise not only changes your body, it changes your mind, your attitude, and your mood." – Unknown

Embarking on the path of physical wellness, we discover a powerful ally in the fight against anxiety: exercise. This section explores how regular physical activity, much like a rhythmic dance, can be a harmonious melody for the mind and body, effectively alleviating anxiety and lifting our spirits.

Imagine your body as an instrument and exercise as the art of playing it. Each movement, each rhythm, contributes to a symphony that resonates with vitality and tranquillity.

The Steady Beat of Consistency: The key to unlocking the benefits of exercise lies in its regularity. Aim for a consistent rhythm in your physical activities, integrating moderate exercise into your daily routine. This consistency helps in building endurance and resilience, both physically and mentally.

Harmonising with Joyful Activities: Choose forms of exercise that spark joy within you. This could be the gentle flow of yoga, the energetic steps of a dance, the refreshing strokes of swimming, or the simple pleasure of a walk in nature. When exercise is enjoyable, it doesn't feel like a chore; instead, it becomes a cherished part of your day.

Mind and Body in Unison: Engage in activities that unite mindfulness with movement. Practices like yoga and tai chi are not just about physical fitness; they are meditations in motion. This fusion of mind and body nurtures a deep sense of calm and presence, amplifying the anxiety-reducing effects of exercise.

Releasing the Endorphin Symphony: Understand the science behind the magic. Exercise releases endorphins, your body's natural mood lifters. These endorphins play a melody of happiness in your brain, reducing stress and improving your mood.

Tuning into Nature's Rhythm: Whenever possible, exercise outdoors. The synergy of physical activity and connecting with nature can be incredibly therapeutic, enhancing the anxiety-reducing benefits of your workout.

Creating a Balanced Routine: Incorporate a variety of activities into your exercise routine. A balance of cardiovascular exercises, strength training, and flexibility workouts ensures a holistic approach to physical and mental health.

Listening to Your Body's Tempo: Pay attention to your body's needs and limits. Exercise should be invigorating, not exhausting. Listen to your body's signals and adjust your activities accordingly.

Through the empowering practice of regular exercise, you orchestrate a rhythm that not only strengthens your body but also calms your mind. It's a journey of discovering the joy in movement, the peace in exertion, and the serenity in consistency. Let each step, each breath, and each stretch be a note in your personal anthem of well-being.

3. Sleep: Essential for Emotional Regulation

> *"Sleep is the golden chain that ties health and our bodies together." – Thomas Dekker*

In the intricate ballet of life, where each day is filled with its rhythms and movements, sleep stands as a vital interlude, a restorative sanctuary essential for emotional regulation and well-being. This section delves into the art of cultivating healthy sleep habits, exploring how the quality of our slumber profoundly influences our ability to manage anxiety and maintain emotional balance.

Imagine your nightly sleep as a sacred retreat, a time when the body and mind can rest, heal, and rejuvenate. Just as a sanctuary is carefully designed to provide peace, your sleep environment and routines should be meticulously crafted to foster restful slumber.

The Rhythm of Routine: Establishing a consistent sleep routine is like setting a rhythm for your body's internal clock. Strive to go to bed and wake up at the same time every day, even on weekends. This regularity harmonises your body's sleep-wake cycle, making it easier to fall asleep and wake up naturally.

Designing Your Sleep Sanctuary: Transform your bedroom into a haven conducive to sleep. Ensure it's dark, cool, and quiet – a cocoon that shields you from the world's hustle. Consider using blackout curtains, earplugs, or white noise machines to create an optimal sleep environment.

The Final Curtain on Screen Time: In the hour before bed, draw the curtain on all electronic devices. The blue light emitted by screens can disrupt your natural sleep cycle, tricking your brain into thinking it's still daytime. Instead, engage in calming activities like reading a book or listening to soft music.

Embrace Pre-Sleep Rituals: Develop a pre-sleep ritual that signals your body it's time to wind down. This could be a warm bath, gentle stretches, or a cup of herbal tea. These rituals act as a gentle lullaby for your body and mind.

Mindful Unwinding: If your mind is a whirlwind of thoughts, try a mindfulness exercise or journaling before bed. This practice can help you unload your thoughts and ease into a peaceful state of mind.

Navigating Night-Time Wakefulness: If you find yourself awake in the middle of the night, avoid lying in bed anxious or frustrated. Get up, engage in a quiet, non-stimulating activity, and return to bed when you feel sleepy.

Consulting the Sleep Maestros: If sleep difficulties persist, consider seeking advice from a sleep specialist. They can provide tailored guidance and strategies to improve your sleep quality.

By embracing these practices, you not only enhance the quality of your sleep but also fortify your emotional resilience. Good sleep is not a luxury; it's a cornerstone of emotional and physical health. Let each night be a journey to the sanctuary of slumber, where every hour spent asleep strengthens the foundation of your well-being.

Chapter 10: Coping with Stress
Stress-Reduction Techniques: Finding Calm in the Chaos

Navigating Life's Stresses with Effective Strategies

Managing stress is crucial in reducing anxiety. This chapter of *MINDPLAN* explores practical techniques for stress reduction, including relaxation methods and time management skills.

Relaxation Methods: Unwinding Body and Mind

> *"The greatest weapon against stress is our ability to choose one thought over another." – William James*

In the dynamic symphony of life, with its crescendos of stress and daily demands, relaxation techniques emerge as essential instruments in creating a harmonious balance. This chapter introduces you to the art of unwinding both body and mind, offering a repertoire of relaxation methods designed to lower the body's stress response and cultivate a serene, rejuvenating state of being.

Imagine each relaxation technique as an instrument in an orchestra, each contributing to the overall harmony of your well-being. Learning to play these instruments can transform moments of discord into melodies of calm and tranquillity.

Deep Breathing Exercises: The breath is a powerful conductor of relaxation. Techniques like abdominal breathing or the 4-7-8 method are simple yet profound ways to activate the body's relaxation response. Each deep, controlled breath is a note that soothes the nervous system, signalling peace to the body and mind.

Progressive Muscle Relaxation: This technique is like a systematic symphony, moving through different muscle groups, tensing and then relaxing them. It's a method that teaches the body the contrast between tension and relaxation, often revealing hidden stress in muscles you weren't aware of. The release of tension in each muscle is a chord that resonates with relaxation.

Guided Relaxation: Engage in the soothing narrative of guided relaxation. Whether it's through imagery, such as visualising a tranquil scene, or through guided meditation apps, these narratives lead you on a journey of calm. Listening to these soothing stories or instructions is like following a gentle stream, meandering through landscapes of peace and serenity.

Creating a Relaxation Ritual: Integrate these techniques into a daily or weekly ritual. Just as a musician practices regularly, consistent practice of relaxation techniques enhances their effectiveness and your ability to invoke relaxation at will.

Personalising Your Techniques: Not every relaxation technique will resonate with you. Experiment with different methods to find what works best for you, much like a composer experimenting with different melodies to create the perfect symphony.

Mindful Integration: Incorporate moments of relaxation throughout your day. Take short breaks to engage in deep breathing or visualisation, especially during moments of high stress.

The Role of Environment: Create a conducive environment for relaxation. A quiet, comfortable space can enhance your relaxation practice, making it more effective.

By mastering these relaxation techniques, you create a personal toolkit to combat stress and anxiety. Each method is a note in the melody of your day, contributing to a greater sense of calm and well-being. Embrace these practices, and let them guide you into a state of harmony and tranquillity, where the body and mind can find rest and rejuvenation.

Time Management: Organising for Peace of Mind

"Time is the wisest counsellor of all." – Pericles

In the intricate dance of daily life, where countless tasks and responsibilities vie for our attention, mastering the art of time management becomes an essential skill for achieving harmony and peace of mind. This section guides you through the process of organising your time, transforming chaos into a well-orchestrated symphony that plays to the rhythm of efficiency and tranquillity.

Imagine your daily tasks as musical notes in a grand composition. Without proper arrangement, these notes can clash, creating dissonance and stress. Effective time management is the art of arranging these notes in a harmonious order, ensuring each has its place and time to be played.

Prioritising with Purpose: Utilise tools like the Eisenhower Box to categorise tasks based on their urgency and importance. This is like sorting the musical notes, deciding which should be played first and which can wait. Prioritisation helps you focus on what truly matters, reducing the stress of trying to play every note at once.

Breaking Down the Composition: Large, complex tasks can be overwhelming. Break them down into smaller, more manageable steps. This approach turns a complicated symphony into individual, easy-to-play sections, making the overall task less daunting and more achievable.

Setting the Tempo with Realistic Goals: Be mindful of your capacity and set achievable goals. Over commitment is like trying to play a complex musical piece at an impossible speed. Understand your limits and set a tempo that is challenging yet manageable.

The Power of Saying No: Learn to decline tasks that are beyond your capacity or don't align with your priorities. Saying no is not a sign of weakness; it's an act of defining your boundaries. It ensures you don't take on more notes than you can handle, keeping your symphony balanced and beautiful.

Harmonising Tasks: Find ways to harmonise tasks, combining or streamlining where possible. This might involve grouping similar tasks together or finding efficient ways to handle routine chores.

Embracing Flexibility: While structure is important, so is flexibility. Be prepared to adjust your schedule as new tasks or unforeseen challenges arise. Flexibility allows you to adapt your symphony in response to life's unpredictable rhythms.

Regular Reviews: Periodically review your time management strategies. What's working well? What can be improved? This review is like fine-tuning your instruments, ensuring they continue to produce the desired sound.

By mastering the art of time management, you transform your daily routine into a harmonious symphony of productivity and peace. Each task is given its due time and importance, reducing the rush and stress of last-minute scrambles. This orchestration of time not only enhances your efficiency but also creates a more balanced and fulfilling life.

Resilience Building: Cultivating Strength to Overcome Stress

Forging a Mind-set for Endurance and Recovery

Resilience, the ability to bounce back from stress and adversity, is a crucial skill in managing anxiety. This section delves into strategies for building resilience, empowering you to handle life's challenges with greater ease and confidence.

1. Understanding Resilience

"Do not judge me by my success, judge me by how many times I fell down and got back up again." – Nelson Mandela

In the journey of life, strewn with its inevitable ups and downs, resilience stands as a towering beacon of strength and adaptability. This section is dedicated to understanding resilience, not as a shield against adversity, but as a skill in navigating through and growing from life's challenges.

Imagine resilience as the process of alchemy, turning the lead of stress and adversity into the gold of wisdom and strength. It's about understanding that the fires of difficulty can forge greater endurance and flexibility in us.

Embracing Emotional Endurance: Recognise that resilience is rooted in emotional endurance. It's not about not feeling the impact of stress or pain, but about experiencing these emotions and persisting through them. Like a tree that bends in the storm but doesn't break, resilience is about swaying with the emotional winds and standing tall afterward.

Cultivating Adaptability: Develop the ability to adapt to changing circumstances. This flexibility is like water flowing around obstacles. When faced with change or difficulty, look for new paths and approaches instead of being paralysed by the loss of the familiar.

Learning from Adversity: View every challenge as a learning opportunity. Ask yourself, "What can this experience teach me?" Every setback or hardship carries a lesson, which, when embraced, contributes to your growth and wisdom.

Building a Support System: Resilience doesn't mean going it alone. Forge strong relationships and a support network. The encouragement and perspective of others can be invaluable in times of stress.

Practicing Self-Care: Prioritise self-care and mindfulness practices. Activities like exercise, meditation, and hobbies are not just leisure; they are tools that help maintain your emotional and mental equilibrium.

Setting Realistic Expectations: Understand that resilience is a journey, not a destination. It's about gradual progress, not instantaneous perfection. Be patient and kind to yourself as you navigate this path.

Reflecting and Reassessing: Regularly take time to reflect on your experiences and reactions. Self-reflection is key to understanding your patterns of thought and behaviour, allowing you to cultivate more effective ways of coping.

Seeking Professional Guidance: If building resilience feels overwhelming, consider seeking the help of a therapist or counsellor. Professional guidance can offer strategies and insights that enhance your resilience journey.

By embracing and cultivating resilience, you transform your response to life's challenges. It's about moving from reactivity to proactivity, from being buffeted by the waves of adversity to skilfully surfing them. Resilience is the quiet power that propels you forward, helping you to emerge from each trial stronger, wiser, and more capable.

2. Developing a Positive Outlook

"A pessimist sees the difficulty in every opportunity; an optimist sees the opportunity in every difficulty." – Winston Churchill

In the vibrant tapestry of life, our perspective can dramatically colour our experiences. Now we will delve into the art of developing a positive outlook, a crucial element in the resilience toolkit. It's about learning to view life through a lens of optimism, not to deny the existence of challenges, but to embrace them as catalysts for growth and transformation.

Imagine your perspective as a palette of colours with which you paint your life's experiences. A positive outlook adds vibrant, hopeful hues to this palette, transforming how you perceive and react to life's challenges.

Practicing the Art of Gratitude: Begin each day by acknowledging and appreciating the positive aspects of your life. This could be as simple as the warmth of the sun, the comfort of a home, or the smile of a loved one. Regular gratitude practice shifts your focus from what's missing or problematic to what's abundant and right, colouring your world with a more positive hue.

Reframing the Canvas of Challenges: When faced with obstacles, instead of painting them as insurmountable problems, try to reframe them as opportunities for learning and growth. Ask yourself, "What can this challenge teach me?" This reframe is like choosing to add a stroke of hopeful colour to a seemingly dark scene.

Focusing on the Controllable Elements: In any situation, concentrate on the aspects you can influence or control. This focus empowers you, turning feelings of helplessness into action.

Cultivating Optimism as a Habit: Make optimism a daily practice. This might involve positive affirmations, surrounding yourself with positive influences, or simply choosing to look for the silver lining in difficult situations.

Nurturing a Supportive Environment: Surround yourself with people who uplift and support you. A positive environment reinforces a positive outlook, creating a cycle of optimism and resilience.

Mindful Positivity: Be mindful of your thoughts and language. Cultivate a habit of speaking and thinking in positive terms. This mindfulness acts as a filter, screening out pessimistic noise.

Seeking Inspirational Stories: Draw inspiration from stories of people who have overcome challenges. Their journeys can offer valuable insights and reinforce your belief in the power of a positive outlook.

Embracing Setbacks as Part of the Journey: Understand that setbacks are part of the path to growth. Each setback is a lesson, adding depth and wisdom to your life's portrait.

By developing a positive outlook, you not only enhance your resilience but also enrich the quality of your life. This perspective is not about wearing rose-coloured glasses; it's about choosing to see life's challenges as shades of opportunity, each adding to the beautiful, complex picture of your life.

3. Building Emotional Awareness

> *"The real voyage of discovery consists not in seeking new landscapes, but in having new eyes." – Marcel Proust*

Embarking on the journey of resilience, we soon realise that the compass guiding us through is our emotional awareness. This section is an exploration into understanding and managing your emotions, a critical skill in steering the ship of resilience through the turbulent waters of stress and adversity.

Imagine your emotional world as a vast ocean. Each emotion is a wave, some small and gentle, others large and overwhelming. Emotional awareness is the skill of recognising these waves, understanding their nature, and learning to sail through them with grace and skill.

The Compass of Awareness: Begin by cultivating an acute awareness of your emotions. This is like learning to read the compass of your internal seas. Regularly check in with yourself, acknowledging and naming what you feel – be it anger, sadness, joy, or fear.

Emotional Regulation Techniques: Integrate practices like mindfulness and deep breathing into your daily routine. These techniques are like anchors, helping to keep your emotional ship stable in the midst of stormy seas. They provide a moment of pause, allowing you to respond to emotions with intention rather than being swept away by them.

Understanding the Whys: Dive deeper into understanding why you feel certain emotions. Are they reactions to external events, the result of internal narratives, or echoes of past experiences? This exploration is like charting the depths of your emotional ocean, discovering what lies beneath the surface.

The Art of Reflection: Engage in regular self-reflection. Journaling, meditation, or quiet contemplation can be invaluable tools in processing and understanding your emotions. Reflection is the lighthouse that illuminates the patterns and paths of your emotional landscape.

Practicing Mindful Responses: Train yourself to respond to emotions mindfully rather than reacting impulsively. This practice is like learning to skilfully navigate your ship, choosing the course of action that best aligns with your values and goals.

Seeking Support in Rough Waters: Remember, navigating your emotional world doesn't have to be a solitary journey. Seeking support from friends, family, or a therapist can offer guidance and a different perspective, helping you to understand and manage your emotions more effectively.

Embracing All Weather: Accept that experiencing a wide range of emotions is a part of being human. Instead of resisting certain feelings, learn to embrace them as part of your journey. Each emotion, pleasant or unpleasant, has something to teach.

By building emotional awareness and mastering regulation techniques, you equip yourself with the tools necessary to navigate life's stresses and challenges with resilience. This emotional acuity allows you to not only weather the storms but also to appreciate the calmer waters. It's a journey of becoming an adept sailor on the ever-changing seas of your emotional world.

4. Strengthening Social Connections

"Alone we can do so little; together we can do so much." – Helen Keller

Resilience, often perceived as a solitary journey of inner strength, is in fact deeply rooted in the soil of social connections. This section unveils the critical role of supportive relationships in fostering resilience, highlighting how our bonds with others can be a powerful source of comfort, strength, and belonging, especially during turbulent times.

Imagine your life as a tapestry, with each thread representing a different relationship – family, friends, colleagues, and mentors. The strength and vibrancy of this tapestry lie in the quality and depth of these threads, each one adding to the resilience and beauty of the whole.

Cultivating Meaningful Relationships: Focus on nurturing deep, meaningful relationships. Like tending a garden, these relationships require time, attention, and care. Prioritise spending quality time with loved ones, engaging in honest and open communication, and building trust and understanding.

Seeking Emotional Support: Recognise the value of emotional support from your social network. In times of stress or adversity, the empathy, encouragement, and perspective of others can be a lifeline, offering comfort and helping you navigate through challenges.

Fostering a Sense of Belonging: Engage in communities or groups where you feel a sense of belonging. This could be a club, religious community, support group, or any gathering of individuals with shared interests or experiences. A sense of belonging reinforces your identity and resilience.

Being a Pillar for Others: Just as you draw strength from your relationships, offer the same support to others. Being there for someone else not only strengthens the bond but also reinforces your own sense of purpose and resilience.

Building a Diverse Network: Cultivate a diverse social network. Different people can offer different types of support – some may be great listeners, while others might provide practical help or advice. A diverse network ensures a well-rounded support system.

Practicing Gratitude for Relationships: Regularly express gratitude for the people in your life. Acknowledging the value of your relationships deepens them and enhances your appreciation for the support they provide.

Balance in Relationships: While social connections are vital, it's also important to maintain a balance. Ensure that your relationships are reciprocal and healthy, and avoid over-reliance on others to the point of losing your independence.

By strengthening your social connections, you weave a stronger, more resilient tapestry of life. These connections provide a safety net of emotional support, advice, and belonging, buffering against the storms of stress and adversity. In the symphony of life, each relationship is a beautiful note that contributes to the harmony and resilience of your existence.

5. Practicing Self-Care

"Taking care of yourself doesn't mean me first, it means me too." – L.R. Knost

In the relentless pace of modern life, where stressors and challenges are a constant presence, the practice of self-care emerges as a vital strategy for building and maintaining resilience. Let us explore the multifaceted art of self-care, emphasising its role as a foundational pillar in fostering physical, emotional, and psychological strength.

Imagine your life as a garden. Self-care is the act of tending this garden – watering it, removing weeds, and ensuring it gets enough sunlight. Just as a well-cared-for garden flourishes, a life infused with self-care practices becomes more resilient and vibrant.

The Role of Regular Exercise: Integrate physical activity into your routine. Exercise is like sunlight for your garden; it nourishes and energises your body and mind. Whether it's a brisk walk, a yoga session, or a vigorous workout, regular exercise enhances mood, reduces symptoms of anxiety and depression, and builds physical resilience.

Cultivating Restful Sleep: Prioritise quality sleep. Restful sleep is the night-time fertiliser that rejuvenates your mind and body. Establish a sleep-conducive environment and a consistent bedtime routine to ensure you get adequate, restorative sleep. This rest is essential for emotional balance and mental clarity.

Balanced Nutrition for Strength: Feed your body with balanced, nourishing meals. Like watering your garden, a healthy diet provides the necessary nutrients for your body to function optimally, supporting your resilience against stress and fatigue.

Mindfulness and Relaxation: Incorporate mindfulness and relaxation techniques into your life. Practices like meditation, deep breathing, or even a relaxing bath can help calm your mind, reduce stress, and enhance mental resilience.

Creating Time for Joy and Relaxation: Make time for activities that bring you joy and relaxation. Engaging in hobbies, spending time in nature, or simply enjoying a quiet moment with a book are crucial for maintaining a balanced and resilient spirit.

Setting Boundaries for Wellness: Learn to set boundaries in both your personal and professional life. Recognising and respecting your limits prevents burnout and ensures you have the energy to care for yourself.

By embracing and practicing self-care, you not only enhance your ability to cope with stress but also cultivate a life of balance and well-being. Self-care is not a luxury; it is a necessity – a fundamental practice that empowers you to meet life's challenges with strength, grace, and resilience.

Work-Life Balance: Harmonising Your Professional and Personal Life

Creating Equilibrium in a Demanding World

Achieving a healthy work-life balance is essential for reducing stress and enhancing overall well-being. This section offers practical strategies to help you find and maintain this balance, fostering a more fulfilling and less stressful life.

1. Setting Boundaries

"No is a complete sentence." – Anne Lamott

In the intricate dance of balancing professional ambitions with personal well-being, the skill of setting boundaries emerges as a critical step in the choreography. This section explores the art of establishing and maintaining clear boundaries between work and life, a practice that fosters harmony, reduces stress, and enhances overall satisfaction.

Imagine your life as a sculptor's studio, where each area of work and personal life is a different piece of art. Setting boundaries is like creating distinct spaces for each sculpture, ensuring that the tools and materials of one do not clutter and disrupt the creation of another.

Carving Out Work Hours: Define your work hours with clarity and commitment. These hours are the frame within which the professional part of your life operates. Resist the temptation to extend these hours unnecessarily, as overstepping this boundary can lead to burnout and a diminished personal life.

Creating a Sanctuary of Separation: If working from home, establish a physical space dedicated solely to work. This space is your studio, where professional tasks come to life. When work is done, step out of this space as a symbolic gesture of leaving work behind, transitioning to personal life.

The Mental Switch: Cultivate the ability to mentally switch off from work once your workday concludes. This transition is like changing costumes, shedding the professional role and stepping into personal life with presence and openness.

The Power of 'No': Develop the courage to say no to work demands that infringe upon your personal time. Saying no is an affirmation of your worth and a declaration of your commitment to balance.

Regular Check-Ins: Periodically assess the effectiveness of your boundaries. Are they being respected by others and yourself? Are they helping you achieve balance? This reflection is essential for maintaining the integrity of your boundaries.

Communicating Your Boundaries: Clearly communicate your boundaries to colleagues, clients, and superiors. Transparency helps in managing expectations and reinforces your commitment to these boundaries.

Embracing Flexibility Within Frameworks: While maintaining boundaries is crucial, allow for flexibility when necessary. Life is unpredictable, and sometimes professional and personal spheres might need to overlap temporarily.

Celebrating the Harmony Achieved: Acknowledge and celebrate the balance you achieve through these boundaries. Recognising the positive impact on your well-being and productivity reinforces the value of this practice.

By mastering the art of setting boundaries, you create a harmonious balance between your professional achievements and personal fulfilment. These boundaries are not barriers; they are the thoughtful delineations that allow each aspect of your life to flourish in its own space, contributing to the overall beauty of your life's work.

2. Prioritising Tasks

> *"The key is not to prioritise what's on your schedule, but to schedule your priorities." – Stephen Covey*

In the rhythmic ballet of daily life, where time is the music to which we all move, mastering the art of prioritising tasks is akin to choreographing a graceful dance. This section delves into the strategy of efficient task management, both in the professional and personal realms, to prevent the sensation of being overwhelmed and to carve out time for the things that truly matter.

Imagine your tasks as dancers in a performance. Some must take the stage now, while others can wait in the wings. The art of prioritisation is like being the director of this performance, deciding who dances when, ensuring the show runs smoothly without any performer being overburdened.

Composing Priority Lists: Start by creating lists that distinguish between tasks based on urgency and importance. This categorisation is like setting the sequence of a dance routine – understanding which steps need to be executed first and which can follow. Focus on what requires immediate attention (urgent and important) and identify tasks that, while important, may not require immediate action.

The Art of Delegation: Recognise the power of delegation both at work and home. Delegating tasks effectively is like assigning parts of the dance to the right performers. Identify tasks that others can handle and entrust them with these responsibilities. This not only ensures the task is completed but also frees you to focus on tasks that require your specific skills or presence.

Balancing the Personal and Professional: Ensure that your prioritisation includes personal activities and downtime. Just as a dance performance includes moments of high energy and periods of rest, your day should balance professional responsibilities with personal care and leisure.

The Rhythm of Routine: Establish routines for recurring tasks. This regularity is like a rehearsed dance sequence that flows smoothly with practice. Routines reduce the mental load of planning and decision-making, allowing for more efficient use of time.

Tuning into Flexibility: While prioritisation is crucial, so is flexibility. Be prepared to adjust your plans as new tasks emerge or circumstances change. This flexibility allows you to adapt your dance to the changing rhythm of the day.

Reflecting on Your Choreography: Regularly review your approach to prioritising tasks. Reflect on what's working and what's not. Are you spending your time on the most important tasks? Are you maintaining a balance between work and personal life? This reflection helps in fine-tuning your strategy.

By mastering the art of prioritising tasks, you choreograph a dance that balances efficiency with fulfilment. This practice enables you to navigate through your days with a sense of control and accomplishment, ensuring that you're not just busy, but productive and content.

3. The Art of Saying No

"The difference between successful people and really successful people is that really successful people say no to almost everything." – Warren Buffett

In the intricate dance of life, where each step represents a commitment or task, the ability to gracefully say 'no' is akin to mastering a powerful yet subtle dance move. This section is dedicated to the art of saying no – a skill crucial for maintaining balance in life, managing your workload, and avoiding the pitfalls of over commitment.

Imagine your life as a dance floor, with each invitation to engage in a task or commitment as an invitation to dance. Not every song is yours to dance to. Learning to say no is about choosing the tunes that resonate with your rhythm and politely declining the rest.

Evaluating the Invitation to Dance: Before you agree to take on additional tasks or commitments, pause and evaluate. Does this request align with your priorities and goals? Do you have the time and energy to commit to it without compromising your existing responsibilities? This evaluation is like listening to the song and deciding whether it fits your dance style and energy.

Clear and Respectful Communication: When you decide to decline, communicate your decision clearly and assertively, yet with respect. It's like declining a dance invitation with grace – there's no need for elaborate excuses, just a simple and respectful, "Thank you, but I won't be able to commit to this."

Practicing the Refusal Routines: Saying no can be uncomfortable, especially if you're not used to it. Practice this skill in less high-stakes situations to build your confidence. Each practice is a rehearsal for the more challenging performances.

Understanding the Value of Your Time: Recognise that your time is a precious resource. Every yes to something is a no to something else. Guard your time like a treasure, and only spend it on commitments that are truly valuable to you.

Setting Boundaries with Elegance: Saying no is an essential part of setting healthy boundaries. These boundaries are like the edges of the dance floor – they define your space and what you are willing to engage in.

The Guilt-Free Decline: Often, saying no is accompanied by guilt. Work on letting go of this guilt. Remember, by saying no to one thing, you're saying yes to something else that's important to you.

The Art of Delegation: In some cases, you can delegate the task or find an alternative solution. This is like finding another dancer who's excited about the tune and ready to take the floor.

By mastering the art of saying no, you choreograph a life dance that is more harmonious and aligned with your values and capabilities. This skill not only prevents burnout but also allows you to dedicate yourself fully to the commitments you choose to engage with. Saying no is not just a refusal; it's an affirmation of your priorities and a step towards a more balanced and fulfilling life.

4. Taking Breaks and Downtime

"Almost everything will work again if you unplug it for a few minutes, including you." – Anne Lamott

In the relentless pursuit of productivity and the continuous juggling of life's responsibilities, the wisdom of incorporating regular breaks and downtime emerges as a crucial melody in the symphony of a balanced life. This section is an ode to the art of rest, highlighting the importance of pauses both during the workday and in personal life, and how they contribute to overall well-being, productivity, and happiness.

Imagine your daily routine as a piece of music. While the notes represent tasks and activities, the rests – the silences between the notes – are equally important. These pauses enhance the music's beauty and prevent it from becoming a discordant jumble of noise.

Scheduling Short Interludes: Incorporate short, scheduled breaks throughout your workday. These interludes are like the rests in a piece of music, giving you a moment to breathe and reset. A five-minute walk, a brief meditation, or simply stepping away from your desk can revitalise your mind, boost productivity, and mitigate stress.

Planning Personal Downtime: Ensure that your personal life includes periods of downtime. This is your time to engage in activities that bring you joy, relaxation, and rejuvenation. Whether it's reading a book, pursuing a hobby, or spending time in nature, these activities are the counterbalance to your work and responsibilities.

The Art of Doing Nothing: Learn to appreciate the art of doing nothing. In a culture that glorifies busyness, standing still can feel unnatural. Yet, it is in these quiet moments of stillness that we often find our deepest sense of peace and clarity.

Quality over Quantity: Focus on the quality of your breaks rather than the quantity. Even a few minutes of genuine, mindful relaxation can be more refreshing than hours spent in aimless leisure.

Digital Detox: During breaks, consider a digital detox. Disconnecting from phones, emails, and social media can significantly enhance the quality of your rest, allowing you to return to your tasks with renewed focus and energy.

Respecting the Need for Rest: Recognise and respect your need for breaks. Just as a musician respects the pauses in a score, understand that rest is an integral part of your productivity and well-being.

Creating Restful Rituals: Develop rituals around your breaks and downtime. This could be a cup of tea during your afternoon break or a weekend walk in the park. Rituals give you something to look forward to and help in creating a restful mind-set.

By embracing the practice of taking breaks and scheduling downtime, you compose a life that balances activity with rest, engagement with relaxation. This balance is the key to sustaining long-term productivity, happiness, and health. Let each break be a note of silence that adds depth and richness to the melody of your life.

Chapter 11: Building Resilience and Positivity

Here, we'll delve into the heart of building resilience and positivity. Think of this chapter as your personal toolkit for cultivating an unshakeable inner strength and a perspective that sees the glass as half full, even during challenging times.

The Essence of Resilience

Envision resilience as an invisible shield, a powerful protector against the unpredictability of life. Understanding and cultivating resilience can transform the way you navigate life's challenges, providing a steadfast anchor amidst the ever-changing tides.

Every obstacle in your path is not just a hurdle to overcome but a unique opportunity to fortify your inner strength. This book guides you on how to convert struggles into powerful catalysts for personal growth and development. You'll learn strategies to transform adversity into a foundation upon which you can build a more resilient, empowered self.

Just as physical muscles grow stronger with exercise, your emotional resilience flourishes with consistent practice and training. Discover a range of emotional exercises designed to enhance your capacity to recover from setbacks and emotional upheavals. These practices will equip you with the skills to remain poised and composed, even in the face of life's unexpected emotional challenges. Let's embark on this journey of building emotional resilience, turning it into a robust shield that guards and empowers you through all of life's experiences.

The Art of Positive Living

In the vibrant canvas of positive living, cultivating a sunshine mind-set is more than just acknowledging the good; it's about finding joy and opportunity even amidst life's inevitable storms. This book delves into the transformative power of positive thinking, demonstrating how it can reshape your day-to-day reality. We explore how to embrace positivity, not by overlooking life's challenges, but by learning to thrive within them.

Embarking on the gratitude path is a journey of recognising and appreciating the small wonders of everyday life. We'll discover how daily practices of gratitude, even in their simplicity, can lead to significant shifts in how you perceive and interact with the world around you.

Equally crucial is the art of realistic optimism. This approach teaches you to blend hope with a grounded sense of reality. Understanding and practicing this balance is key to cultivating a sustainable, positive outlook on life. Through these pages, we'll explore strategies and exercises that help you build a life filled with positivity, gratitude, and realistic optimism. This is your journey towards creating a life where you don't just endure the rain but learn to dance in it with joy and resilience.

Social Roots of Resilience and Positivity

In the quest for resilience and positivity, the roots often lie within our social connections. In this section, we delve into the pivotal role that strong, supportive relationships play in fostering resilience. Understand that you are not an isolated entity; your strength often comes from the network of connections around you. We will explore effective strategies to cultivate and nurture these vital relationships, recognising that they are essential pillars in your life's journey.

Moreover, embracing community spirit offers a dual benefit. As you engage and connect with your community, you not only bolster your own resilience but also contribute significantly to the well-being of those around you. This reciprocal relationship between giving and receiving support is a fundamental component of a truly fulfilling life. Through practical advice and real-life examples, this book will guide you in strengthening your social roots, teaching you how to create and maintain relationships and community connections that enrich both your life and the lives of others.

Developing a Resilient Mind-Set: Techniques to foster resilience

Think of resilience not just as a skill but as an art; an art that you're about to master. It's about crafting an inner core of strength that stands unwavering in the face of life's storms.

The Resilience Recipe

Acceptance:

The journey towards resilience begins with a crucial step: acceptance. Embracing acceptance means understanding that life is a tapestry woven with both joys and challenges. Acceptance isn't synonymous with defeat or complacency; rather, it's a courageous acknowledgement of reality. It's about recognising that while you may not have control over certain situations, your power lies in how you respond to them.

Acceptance is often misunderstood as resignation, but there's a significant difference. It's not about passively enduring hardships, but rather about facing them with clarity and a sense of realism. When you accept a challenge, you stop expending energy on denying or fighting the unchangeable and start focusing on actionable steps you can take.

This acceptance forms the bedrock upon which resilience is built. It's the steady ground from which you can start to assess, plan, and act. From this vantage point, you're better positioned to tackle challenges effectively, learning from them, and moving forward with greater wisdom and strength.

Optimism:

Optimism is the light that guides you through the dark tunnels of hardship. It's not about wearing rose-coloured glasses and ignoring the gravity of situations, but about maintaining a belief that positive outcomes are possible, even in tough times.

Optimistic resilience is a balance between realism and hope. It's understanding that while life can be difficult, these difficulties are not the entirety of your experience. By maintaining an optimistic outlook, you empower yourself to seek solutions and opportunities even in the face of adversity.

Optimism is the art of spotting silver linings in every cloud, no matter how faint they may appear. It's the ability to see beyond the immediate pain or setback and recognise the potential for growth and learning. This positive perspective doesn't diminish the challenge, but it does change how you interact with it. An optimistic mind set encourages resilience by fostering a sense of hope and possibility, making you more resilient in the face of life's inevitable challenges.

You can cultivate optimism by practicing gratitude, engaging in positive self-talk, and surrounding yourself with supportive and positive influences. Remember, optimism isn't a naïve dismissal of reality, but a choice to focus on what can be rather than what can't.

Incorporating acceptance and optimism into your life creates a powerful recipe for resilience. These ingredients, when combined, provide the strength and perspective needed to navigate life's challenges with grace and determination. They allow you to bounce back from setbacks and emerge stronger, wiser, and more capable.

Building Emotional Muscles

Building resilience is akin to building physical strength – it requires regular practice and dedication. Just as you would go to a gym to strengthen your body, there are mental 'exercises' you can engage in to fortify your emotional resilience.

One of the most effective exercises for emotional strength is mindfulness meditation. Think of it as weightlifting for your mind. Just as lifting weights builds physical muscle, mindfulness

[134]

meditation strengthens your ability to remain calm and focused amidst life's chaos.

It involves practicing awareness of the present moment, acknowledging thoughts and feelings without judgment, and gently guiding your focus back to the here and now. This practice enhances your ability to remain cantered and calm, even when external circumstances are challenging.

Incorporate regular 'workouts' for your emotional muscles. This could include daily mindfulness sessions, journaling to process and understand emotions, or engaging in reflective practices like gratitude or affirmations. Over time, these practices build your emotional resilience, much like regular physical exercise builds physical stamina and strength.

The Power of Perspective

The lens through which you view life's challenges significantly impacts your resilience. Changing your perspective can transform obstacles into opportunities, a process akin to swapping a pair of gloomy glasses for ones that bring clarity and positivity.

Learn to reframe challenges as opportunities for growth and learning. When faced with a difficult situation, instead of asking "Why is this happening to me?" try asking, "What can I learn from this?" or "How can this experience help me grow?" This shift in perspective doesn't minimise the difficulty of the situation but empowers you to find meaning and potential growth in it.

Cultivate cognitive flexibility – the ability to adapt your thinking in response to changing circumstances. This mental agility allows you to view situations from different angles, consider various solutions, and maintain a more balanced and optimistic outlook. Like flexibility in physical exercise, cognitive flexibility in emotional resilience helps you to bend without breaking.

Choosing an optimistic perspective doesn't mean ignoring life's problems. Instead, it means maintaining a belief in your ability to cope and a hope for positive outcomes. It's like putting on a pair of glasses that help you see the path ahead more clearly, even in the midst of a storm.

Building your emotional muscles through practices like mindfulness and shifting your perspective equips you with the strength and agility to handle life's challenges with greater ease and confidence. It's a journey of becoming stronger, not just on the outside, but on the inside, where it truly counts.

Cultivating a Growth Mind-set

The transformation from a fixed mind-set to a growth mind-set is a pivotal shift in your journey toward resilience and personal development. In a fixed mind-set, abilities and intelligence are seen as static, leading to a desire to appear smart and a tendency to avoid challenges. However, embracing a growth mind-set opens a world of possibilities.

With a growth mind-set, every experience, be it success or failure, is viewed as a learning opportunity. It's a shift from focusing on proving yourself to improving yourself. In this mind-set, failure is not a label but a temporary state, a stepping stone on the path to success. Remember, it's not about how many times you fall, but how many times you rise. Each setback is a chance to learn, grow, and come back stronger.

Adopting a growth mind-set means embracing resilience. When you believe that you can develop and improve, you're more likely to persevere through difficulties. This belief in your ability to grow and adapt is at the heart of resilience.

The journey of cultivating a growth mind-set is synonymous with embracing lifelong learning. It's about nurturing curiosity and maintaining an open mind in the face of new challenges and experiences.

Let curiosity be your guide. Be inquisitive about the world around you, ask questions, and seek to understand. This constant quest for knowledge not only enriches your life but also strengthens your mental flexibility, allowing you to adapt and thrive in various situations.

View every new piece of knowledge or skill as a tool in your resilience toolkit. Whether it's learning from a book, a person, or an experience, each new insight adds to your ability to handle life's ups and downs. This continuous accumulation of knowledge and skills builds a robust foundation for resilience.

Part of learning is being open to new ideas and perspectives, even those that challenge your current beliefs. This openness is a hallmark of a growth mind-set and is crucial for personal and emotional growth. It allows you to see possibilities where others see obstacles and to find solutions in the face of challenges.

Cultivating a growth mind-set is a transformative process that empowers you to view life's challenges as opportunities for growth and learning. It encourages you to persist in the face of setbacks and to see effort as a path to mastery. By embracing this mind-set, you equip yourself with the resilience and flexibility needed to navigate the complexities of life with confidence and optimism.

Resilience in Action

Small Steps, Big Leaps

Developing resilience is a journey best taken one step at a time. Just as a marathon runner doesn't start by running 26.2 miles on the first day, building resilience starts with facing small challenges and gradually increasing your capacity to handle more significant stressors.

Begin by identifying small, manageable challenges in your daily life. This could be as simple as speaking up in a meeting, trying a new activity, or setting a boundary with someone. Each small challenge you overcome builds your confidence and resilience, much like each mile run strengthens a marathoner.

As you successfully navigate these smaller challenges, your resilience grows. You'll find that over time, you're able to handle increasingly difficult situations with greater ease. This process is akin to training muscles – with regular exercise, they become stronger and more capable.

Maintaining a resilience journal can be a profoundly effective tool in your journey. It serves not only as a record of your experiences but also as a reflection of your growth and development over time.

In your resilience journal, note down the challenges you face, how you reacted to them, and what the outcomes were. Be honest and comprehensive in your entries. This practice helps you to objectively look at how you handle stress and adversity, providing insights into your coping mechanisms and areas for improvement.

After each challenge, reflect on what you learned from the experience. Did you discover a new strength? Did you learn something about your limits? Perhaps you found a new strategy for handling stress. Recording these learnings reinforces them in your mind, making it easier to apply them in the future.

Over time, your resilience journal will become a narrative of your personal growth. You'll be able to look back and see how far you've come, which is incredibly empowering. It's a tangible reminder that growth is a process and that you are continually evolving and strengthening your resilience.

Don't forget to celebrate your successes, no matter how small. Acknowledging and celebrating your progress is crucial for maintaining motivation and continuing your resilience journey.

Incorporating these practices of taking small steps and maintaining a resilience journal into your life empowers you to see resilience in action. It's a journey of incremental progress, self-discovery, and continuous growth, leading to a stronger, more resilient you.

Positive Psychology: Harnessing the Power of a Sunny Mind

The Strength of Positive Thoughts

Positive thinking is not just an optimistic attitude; it's a powerful mental tool, a superpower that you can harness in your everyday life. It's the ability to consistently find the silver lining in difficult situations, to see solutions where others see only problems. Like any muscle in your body, this positive mind-set strengthens with practice and dedication.

Cultivating a positive mind-set involves consciously choosing to focus on the positive aspects of a situation, even when facing challenges. It's about training your mind to shift from a default state of finding faults or limitations to one of discovering possibilities and solutions.

Positive thinking contributes significantly to resilience. When you approach life with an optimistic mind-set, you're more likely to persevere through challenges and bounce back from setbacks. This mental fortitude is a key component of resilience, empowering you to navigate life's ups and downs with grace and determination.

Positive Affirmations

Affirmations are powerful tools in reinforcing positive thinking. These short, powerful statements are designed to manifest a specific goal or encourage a positive mind-set.

Phrases like "I am capable," "I am strong," and "I am worthy" are more than just words; they are potent declarations of your inner truth and potential. When repeated consistently, they can shift your mind-set, boost your confidence, and strengthen your belief in your abilities.

Integrate affirmations into your daily routine: Repeat them during moments of doubt or stress, or make them a part of your morning ritual to start your day with positivity and strength.

Positive Psychology in Your Pocket

If I were to ask you to name 10 negative things that happened today, I'm sure you would reel them off quite quickly. However, if I were to you to name 10 positive things that happened today, you'd probably struggle at 2. This isn't because more negative things happen than positive. It's because we focus so much on the things that go wrong, we miss the things that go right.

Therefore, carrying a small notebook dedicated to recording positive experiences can be a transformative practice. This simple tool encourages you to look for, notice and appreciate the positive moments in your life, no matter how small.

Whenever you experience something that brings you joy, jot it down in your Joy Journal. It could be a kind gesture from a stranger, a personal achievement, or a moment of beauty in nature.

Regularly reflecting on these entries not only boosts your mood but also reinforces a positive outlook on life. Over time, this journal becomes a treasure trove of happy memories, a tangible reminder of the joy and positivity that exist in your life.

The Positivity Challenge

Challenge yourself daily to transform a negative thought into a positive one. This practice is like tending to a garden in your mind, where you consciously remove weeds (negative thoughts) and cultivate flowers (positive thoughts) in their place.

When you catch yourself entertaining a negative thought, pause and reframe it into something positive. For instance, if you think, "I can't do this," transform it into, "I will do my best and learn from this experience."

Over time, this daily challenge reshapes your mental landscape, creating an environment where positivity thrives. It's a practice that not only enhances your mood and outlook but also contributes to an overall sense of well-being and happiness.

Coping Strategies for Tough Times: Navigating Life's Stormy Seas

Steering Through Life's Storms with Grace and Strength

Consider this section as your compass and lifeboat, offering practical tips and strategies to help you sail through tough times with resilience and poise.

Embracing the Storm

Embracing the storm means first acknowledging the whirlwind of emotions that tough times inevitably bring. Whether it's fear, sadness, or frustration, understanding that it's completely okay to feel these emotions is paramount. Recognising and accepting your feelings is not a sign of weakness, but the first crucial step in managing them effectively.

In the midst of these challenges lies hidden wisdom. Each difficulty you encounter is an opportunity for learning and growth. When faced with adversity, ask yourself, "What can I learn from this situation?" Adopting this perspective doesn't just aid in coping with the immediate challenge; it transforms these experiences into valuable stepping stones for personal development. This approach allows you to navigate through life's storms not just with resilience but with an evolving sense of self-awareness and strength.

Your Coping Toolkit

Developing a robust coping toolkit is essential for navigating the ebbs and flows of everyday challenges. One of the most powerful tools in this arsenal is staying connected. Reach out to friends, family, or support groups. Engaging in conversations, sharing your thoughts and burdens not only helps in lightening your load but also opens doors to insights and guidance from others. The wisdom and support of those around you can often serve as a beacon of hope and direction in tougher times.

Equally important in your coping toolkit is the development of a self-care routine. Prioritise activities that rejuvenate both your body and spirit. It could be immersing yourself in a good book, taking a leisurely walk, indulging in a hobby, or simply enjoying moments of quiet. Remember, self-care is far from selfish; it's a fundamental component of your overall well-being. It's about giving yourself the permission to pause and engage in activities that bring you joy and relaxation.

The Power of Flexibility

Be like water – adaptable and flexible. When plans go sideways, be open to new directions and solutions. Flexibility is a superpower in tough times.

Create a Plan B: Having a backup plan can ease anxiety about the future. It's like having a life jacket on your boat, just in case.

Finding Calm in the Chaos

In the swirling whirlwind of life's chaos, finding your inner calm is akin to discovering a sanctuary of peace. Mindfulness and meditation stand as beacons in this turmoil, guiding you to anchor in the present moment. These practices are your lighthouses, shining through the fog of chaos, offering calm and clarity. They teach you to pause, reflect, and connect with the tranquillity that lies beneath the surface of your daily hustle.

Equally powerful in this journey is the art of deep breathing – a technique often underestimated in its simplicity yet profound in its impact. It's a direct pathway to tranquillity, a tool readily available at any moment. Each deep breath is a step towards calming your mind and steadying your heart.

Staying Hopeful and Positive

Cultivating an attitude of optimism is like nurturing a garden of hope within you. It's about maintaining a perspective that is anchored in hopefulness and recognising the strength that resides in you. Remind yourself of the challenges you've already overcome and the victories you've achieved. These are not just memories; they are proof of your resilience and capability. You have navigated through storms before, and with each one, you've grown stronger and more adept.

Alongside this optimism, the practice of positive affirmations can be a powerful tool in reinforcing your inner fortitude. Simple yet impactful phrases like "I am resilient" and "I can handle this" serve as mantras that can carry you through tough times. These affirmations are more than words; they are declarations of your strength and resilience.

Chapter 12: Cultivating Positive Habits
Introduction to Positive Habit Formation

The journey of personal transformation is often paved with the bricks of habitual actions. Habits, those repetitive behaviours that we perform almost unconsciously, wield immense power over our daily lives. They are the subtle architects of our destiny, quietly shaping our routines, influencing our decisions, and, ultimately, sculpting our character.

In this chapter, we delve into the heart of positive habit formation. It's about recognising that every small, repeated action is a thread in the larger tapestry of our existence. The power of habits lies in their subtlety and their ability to operate below the surface of our conscious awareness. These automatic responses and behaviours, when aligned positively, can significantly transform the contours of our daily lives.

Understanding the nature of habits is pivotal. They are not just mindless routines but potent tools that shape our mental and physical well-being. By identifying the patterns that drive our actions, we unlock the potential to harness the power of habits to foster positive change and growth. This chapter is dedicated to exploring how, through a solution-focused approach, we can shift from unproductive patterns to empowering routines. It's about setting the stage for a journey of positive transformation, where every step is a conscious move towards a better self.

The Power of Habits

Habits are the invisible threads that weave the fabric of our daily lives. They operate in the background, often below the level of our conscious awareness, yet they hold immense power over our actions and, ultimately, our destiny. These automatic responses and behaviours, which seem trivial when viewed in isolation, cumulatively shape the contours of our existence.

At their core, habits are our brain's way of saving effort. Once a behaviour becomes a habit, it moves into the realm of automaticity, requiring less cognitive load and energy. This efficiency is beneficial, allowing us to perform many of our daily tasks without expending significant mental effort. However, this automatic nature also means that habits, once formed, can be challenging to break.

Recognising the patterns that underlie our habits is the first step towards harnessing their power. Each habit, whether it's reaching for a snack at a certain time of day or automatically checking a smartphone upon waking, is driven by a pattern that has been etched into our neural pathways. These patterns consist of three components: a cue that triggers the behaviour, the routine of the behaviour itself, and the reward that the behaviour delivers.

Understanding these components allows us to dissect our habits, giving us the leverage to change them. For instance, if a habit is triggered by stress (the cue), and the routine is eating unhealthy snacks, resulting in a temporary feeling of relief (the reward), recognising this pattern enables us to intervene and alter it. Perhaps by substituting the routine with a healthier response, like a brief walk or meditation, we can achieve a similar, if not better, reward.

The power of habits extends beyond individual behaviours to impact our mental and physical well-being. Good habits, such as regular exercise or mindful eating, contribute to better health and increased happiness. Conversely, negative habits can lead to a downward spiral, affecting our health, productivity, and overall quality of life.

In a solution-focused approach, the emphasis is not on dwelling on the negative habits but rather on identifying and cultivating positive ones. By shifting our focus from what is lacking to what can be developed, we empower ourselves to make meaningful changes. This perspective encourages us to actively engage in the process of positive habit formation, directing our efforts towards behaviours that promote mental health and overall well-being.

Solution-Focused Perspective

Embracing a solution-focused perspective is a paradigm shift in the journey of personal development, especially when it comes to habit formation. This approach pivots our attention away from dwelling on problems and redirects it towards building what works. In the context of habit formation, it's about shifting our gaze from our deficiencies to our potential for growth and positive change.

This perspective is rooted in the belief that everyone has the capacity for positive change. It's an empowering viewpoint that encourages us to look for strengths and successes, no matter how small, and build upon them. When applied to habits, it means focusing on the habits that serve us well and finding ways to reinforce and multiply them.

The solution-focused approach is inherently optimistic. It is based on the idea that by identifying and amplifying positive behaviours, we can offset and eventually replace negative ones. It's about acknowledging the power we have to shape our actions into habits that align with our goals and values.

For instance, if you find that you feel better on days when you exercise, the solution-focused approach would involve identifying what about those days makes it easier to exercise. Is it the time of day? The type of exercise? The company you keep? Once you understand what works, you can replicate these conditions to make exercising a more regular habit.

This approach also encourages us to be proactive in creating positive habits. It involves taking deliberate steps to cultivate new behaviours that promote mental health and overall well-being. For example, if you aim to reduce stress, you might establish a habit of daily meditation or journaling. The key here is to identify habits that contribute to your well-being and actively integrate them into your life.

[146]

The beauty of the solution-focused perspective is that it transforms the process of habit formation from a daunting task to an exciting journey of self-discovery and improvement. It's about actively engaging in the creation of your life narrative, one positive habit at a time.

By developing positive habits, we create a self-reinforcing cycle of positive change. These habits become the building blocks of a more fulfilling life, furthering our journey toward mental wellness and overall happiness.

Understanding Habit Formation

Habit formation is a fascinating interplay between psychology and neurology. It revolves around a three-part process known as the "habit loop," which is fundamental to both developing new habits and changing existing ones. Understanding this loop is critical for anyone looking to harness the power of habits for positive life changes.

The Habit Loop

The Cue: The cue is a trigger that initiates the behaviour. It could be a specific time, location, emotional state, or sequence of events. For example, feeling stressed (cue) might trigger the habit of reaching for comfort food.

The Routine: This is the behaviour itself, which can be physical, mental, or emotional. The routine in the above example would be eating the comfort food.

The Reward: The reward is the benefit or satisfaction gained from the habit. In our example, the reward might be temporary stress relief or a sense of pleasure from the food.

By identifying the components of the habit loop, we gain valuable insight into our behaviours and the ability to modify them. If a habit is undesirable, understanding its cue and reward provides a starting point for change. This understanding is pivotal for both developing new habits and altering existing ones.

Neurological Foundations

Habits are not just behavioural patterns but also neurological ones. They are formed and maintained through a process called neuroplasticity, where our brain's neurons reorganise and strengthen connections in response to new experiences.

When a behaviour is repeated, the neural pathways associated with that behaviour are strengthened, making the action easier and more automatic over time. This neural efficiency is the reason habits can become deeply ingrained and sometimes challenging to change.

Recognising the neurological basis of habits empowers us to strategically shape our habits. Consistently practicing new behaviours can rewire our brain, gradually replacing old habits with new, more positive ones. This understanding opens up a realm of possibility for personal transformation through habit modification.

Strategies for Developing Positive Habits

The journey of forming positive habits is best undertaken through small, incremental steps. This approach focuses on establishing manageable habits that can be easily integrated into daily life, thus reducing the 'overwhelm' often associated with significant changes.

The key to this approach is consistency; even the smallest habits, when practiced regularly, can lead to profound and lasting changes over time. It's about celebrating small victories and using them as a foundation for further progress. For example, if you aim to be more physically active, start with a five-minute daily walk and gradually increase the duration. The consistency of this small habit can set the stage for more substantial changes.

Replacing negative habits involves a similar understanding of the habit loop. To substitute a negative habit, it's crucial first to identify the cue and reward that sustain it. Once these are understood, the strategy involves substituting the negative routine with a positive one that offers a similar reward. This replacement technique requires mindfulness and consistent practice.

For instance, if stress triggers the habit of mindless snacking (the cue), and the reward is a sense of comfort, you might replace the snacking with a brief walk or a few minutes of deep breathing. This new routine can provide a similar sense of relief (the reward), while also fostering a healthier response to stress.

Creating an environment that supports the new habit and removes triggers for the negative one is also beneficial. Over time, this method can effectively rewire the brain's response to the cues, leading to healthier habits.

Maintaining Positive Habits

Maintaining positive habits is as crucial as forming them. This phase of habit formation is where the true test of resilience and commitment comes into play. It involves not just the repetition of desired behaviours but also an understanding of the dynamics of habit maintenance.

Consistency and Patience

Consistency in your actions and routines is the cornerstone of habit maintenance and development. When you engage in a behaviour repeatedly, you are essentially reinforcing the neural pathways in your brain associated with that activity. This reinforcement makes the habit more automatic and ingrained over time, much like a path becomes more defined the more it is walked upon.

Each time you repeat a behaviour, your brain's neural networks that support that habit become stronger and more efficient. This process is akin to building a muscle; the more you use it, the stronger it gets. Consistent behaviour fortifies these neural connections, gradually turning conscious actions into automatic habits.

Embedding new habits into your daily routine greatly enhances their staying power. For instance, if you aim to practice mindfulness, anchoring it to a specific time each day – such as during your morning routine or right before bed – turns it into a predictable and stable part of your day. Over time, this consistency transforms effortful practice into a natural and effortless part of your life.

The journey of habit formation is a marathon, not a sprint. It requires patience, as change is often a gradual process. The key is to recognise that every small step, taken consistently, plays a significant role in building lasting habits.

Embracing the fact that change doesn't happen overnight is crucial. Just as a plant doesn't grow in a day, habits take time to develop and solidify. Patience is the gentle acknowledgement that while progress may be slow, it is happening.

Acknowledge and celebrate every small step you take in your habit formation journey. These small victories are important milestones and serve as motivation to continue. They are reminders that you are moving in the right direction, no matter the pace.

Alongside patience, persistence is vital. There will be days when sticking to your new habit feels challenging, but it's the continued effort despite these challenges that leads to success. Persistence in the face of difficulty is a testament to your commitment to change.

Be prepared to adapt your approach as needed. If a particular habit isn't sticking, consider tweaking your strategy or finding new ways to integrate it into your routine. Flexibility in your approach demonstrates a commitment not just to the habit itself but to the overall goal of self-improvement and growth.

In summary, consistency and patience are the twin pillars of successful habit formation. By integrating new habits into your daily life with regularity and embracing the gradual nature of change, you set the stage for creating lasting and impactful transformations in your life.

Dealing with Setbacks

Setbacks are an inevitable and natural part of the habit formation journey. Rather than viewing them as failures or defeats, it's important to reframe them as opportunities for learning and growth. In the process of building new habits, it's not uncommon to encounter obstacles or to occasionally slip back into old patterns.

Understand that setbacks are a normal part of any change process. Just like learning a new skill, developing a new habit is a journey filled with ups and downs. These challenges do not reflect your ability or worth; they are simply part of the human experience of growth and change.

Each setback is a valuable source of information. It provides insights into what works, what doesn't, and how you might need to adjust your approach. Instead of being discouraged, use these experiences as a way to understand yourself and your habits better.

When you encounter challenges in maintaining new habits, adopting a solution-focused mind-set is crucial. This approach involves actively seeking ways to overcome obstacles and stay on track with your goals.

Sometimes, setbacks can indicate that your initial goals need revisiting. Perhaps they were too ambitious or not clearly defined. Take this opportunity to adjust your goals so they are more achievable and aligned with your current situation.

Don't hesitate to seek support when facing setbacks. This could be from friends, family, a coach, or a support group. Sharing your challenges with others can provide you with new perspectives, encouragement, and practical advice.

Reconnect with the reasons behind adopting the new habit. What benefits were you hoping to achieve? Keeping these motivations in mind can reignite your commitment and help you navigate through tough times.

Focus on taking small, manageable steps forward. Breaking down your goals into smaller tasks can make them feel more achievable and less overwhelming. Celebrate each small success as you make progress.

Cultivate resilience by reminding yourself that setbacks are temporary. Be flexible in your approach and willing to adapt as needed. Resilience is not about never facing setbacks; it's about bouncing back from them.

Be kind to yourself during setbacks. Engage in positive self-talk rather than being critical or harsh. Encourage yourself as you would a friend, recognising your effort and the progress you've made.

In summary, dealing with setbacks is an integral part of the habit formation process. By understanding them, adopting a solution-focused approach, and staying resilient, you can navigate these challenges effectively and stay committed to your path of personal growth and development.

Integrating Habits into Daily Life

The key to successfully adopting new habits lies in integrating them into your daily life in a way that feels natural and sustainable. This process involves weaving new habits into your existing routines in such a way that they become a seamless part of your day.

To integrate a new habit effectively, identify parts of your daily routine where it could naturally fit. For instance, if your goal is to increase physical activity, you might incorporate a short workout session into your morning routine, or opt for a brisk walk during lunch breaks. The idea is to attach the new habit to an activity that is already a part of your daily life, making it easier to remember and stick to.

Consider the transitional moments in your day – times when you shift from one activity to another. These can be ideal opportunities to incorporate a new habit. For example, practicing a few minutes of mindfulness during your commute or doing a quick stretching routine after finishing work can effectively utilise these transition times.

Another effective strategy for habit integration is creating habit chains, linking new habits to established ones. This technique relies on the power of existing behavioural patterns to support new habits.

To build a habit chain, choose a regular part of your routine and attach the new habit to it. For example, if you're trying to develop a habit of reading more, you might choose to read for a few minutes every night before going to sleep. The key is consistency – by consistently following your established routine with the new habit, you create a chain of activities where one naturally leads to the other.

Understanding the cue-routine-reward cycle can also aid in habit formation. Identify a cue (a regular part of your day), attach the new routine (your new habit), and end with a reward (a sense of accomplishment, a small treat, etc.). For example, your morning coffee (cue) can be followed by a ten-minute language learning session (routine), after which you might reward yourself with a few minutes of leisure time.

As you build these chains, reinforce them with positive reinforcement. Acknowledging and celebrating your success in sticking to the new habit will strengthen the habit chain. This positive feedback loop encourages continued adherence to the new routine.

In summary, the integration of new habits into daily life is crucial for long-term adherence and success. By finding ways to seamlessly incorporate them into your existing schedule and creating habit chains, you set the foundation for these new behaviours to become ingrained, automatic parts of your life.

Long-Term Benefits

The true power of maintaining positive habits lies in their cumulative impact over the long term. Each day you engage in positive habits, you're not just making a small change for that day; you're building a foundation for a lifetime of improved well-being.

The consistent practice of positive habits can lead to significant improvements in mental wellness. Over time, habits like mindfulness, regular exercise, and positive thinking contribute to reduced stress levels, enhanced mood, and a greater sense of overall life satisfaction. These mental health benefits can create a positive feedback loop, where improved mental well-being facilitates the maintenance of other healthy habits.

Positive habits also have a profound impact on physical health. Regular physical activity, healthy eating, and adequate sleep can lead to improved energy levels, a stronger immune system, and a decreased risk of chronic diseases. The synergy between mental and physical health is a cornerstone of holistic well-being.

As you cultivate and maintain positive habits, you'll likely notice an increase in productivity and a sense of personal achievement. Healthy routines can improve focus, creativity, and efficiency, allowing you to achieve more in both your personal and professional life.

Recognising and celebrating your progress is an essential part of the journey. It's important to acknowledge the effort and commitment it takes to maintain positive habits, and to celebrate the milestones you reach along the way.

Don't wait for big milestones to recognise your progress. Celebrate the small victories, like choosing a healthy meal over fast food, completing a workout, or successfully managing a stressful situation. These small achievements are the building blocks of long-term change.

Regular reflection on how far you've come can be incredibly motivating. Whether it's through journaling, sharing your achievements with others, or simply taking a moment to appreciate your efforts, recognition of your progress reinforces the value of your ongoing commitment.

Maintaining positive habits is not a static process but a dynamic one that involves continuous effort, adaptation, and self-compassion.

Be prepared to adapt your habits as your life changes. Flexibility is key to maintaining habits over the long term. What works for you now may need adjustment in the future, and that's perfectly okay.

[154]

Be kind to yourself, especially during challenging times. Understand that setbacks are part of the process and don't define your overall journey. Self-compassion is a powerful tool in maintaining resilience and motivation.

Consistency, Patience, and Resilience: These three qualities are your allies in ensuring that positive habits become a permanent part of your life. With consistency in your actions, patience in your progress, and resilience in the face of challenges, you pave the way for lasting change and personal growth.

In essence, the long-term benefits of maintaining positive habits are far-reaching, impacting every aspect of your life. By embracing this journey with consistency, adaptability, and self-compassion, you set the stage for a lifetime of health, happiness, and fulfilment.

Empowering Change Through Positive Habits

The journey of cultivating positive habits is more than just about the habits themselves; it's a testament to our capacity for self-directed change and growth. Each step taken in developing and maintaining these habits is a stride towards greater mental wellness and a more fulfilling life.

This process is not merely about the acquisition of new behaviours but about the empowerment and self-mastery they foster. The act of taking control of our habits is in itself a powerful exercise in self-discipline and determination. It's about asserting agency over our lives and making conscious decisions that align with our values and aspirations.

Remember, the transformation begins with small, consistent actions. These habits, when practiced regularly, become the tools for building a life of balance, fulfilment, and well-being. They are the keystones in the architecture of our daily existence, supporting and sustaining our journey towards personal excellence.

Embark on this journey with patience and optimism. Embrace each small victory and learn from every setback. Let these habits be your companions in crafting a healthier, more vibrant you. The path to change is in your hands; each habit, a stepping stone to a better tomorrow.

Your journey of cultivating positive habits is not just a path to improved well-being; it's a journey towards realising your fullest potential.

Chapter 13: Overcoming Negative Thought Patterns

Introduction to Overcoming Negative Thought Patterns

In the quiet corners of our minds, where thoughts both shape and reflect our reality, the presence of negative patterns can often cast long shadows over our daily experiences. These patterns, ingrained and often unnoticed, colour our perceptions, emotions, and decisions, sometimes leading us down paths of pessimism, self-doubt, and fear.

The impact of negative thought patterns is profound and far-reaching. They are like unwelcome background music, continuously playing and subtly influencing the quality of our mental and emotional lives. These patterns, whether they manifest as persistent self-criticism, catastrophic forecasting, or a pervasive sense of pessimism, can significantly affect our mental health, our relationships, and our overall sense of well-being.

Recognising and understanding these patterns is the first, crucial step in a transformative process that empowers us to rewrite the narrative of our inner dialogues. It's about breaking free from the grip of unhelpful and destructive thinking and learning how to cultivate a mind-set that supports growth, resilience, and happiness.

The Origins of Negative Thinking

Imagine your life as a tapestry woven with various experiences. Early life encounters, particularly those tinged with trauma or persistent stress, often plant the seeds of negative thinking. These experiences cast long shadows, imprinting patterns of thought that can linger into adulthood. They are like persistent echoes from your past, shaping how you perceive and react to the world.

Now, consider the broader picture – the societal influences that surround us. Our cultural norms, societal expectations, and the widespread media are like a constant stream of messages, some of which sow ideals that are challenging to meet or expose us to negativity. This exposure can subtly shape our worldviews and self-perceptions, often without us even realising it.

The environment of your upbringing also plays a pivotal role, acting as the soil in which these thought patterns take root. A family environment that is critical or unsupportive can foster seeds of negative self-talk and beliefs. It's like nurturing a garden with the wrong nutrients – the resulting growth is often skewed.

Reflect on your formative years, which can be a fertile ground for negative thought patterns. Experiences of bullying, academic struggles, or social exclusion leave deep imprints, contributing to a lasting legacy of negative thinking. These experiences are like permanent marks on your psyche, influencing how you view yourself and the world around you.

Stress and external pressures act as amplifiers of negativity. Chronic stress, be it from work, relationships, or life's challenges, can intensify negative thinking, tinting your outlook on life with pessimism. The demands and pressures to meet certain standards or achieve specific goals, whether self-imposed or from external sources, can further engrain this pattern of negative thinking. They can especially affect your sense of self-worth and capabilities, like a relentless tide eroding your confidence.

Understanding the origins of your negative thought patterns is not just an exercise in introspection; it's a vital step on your journey towards transformation. This understanding empowers you to address these deep-seated patterns, paving the way for positive change. Remember, this exploration is not about assigning blame but about gaining insight.

Understanding Negative Thought Patterns

Imagine your mind as a garden. Just as a garden can flourish with beautiful flowers or be overrun by weeds, so too can your mind be filled with positive thoughts or negative thought patterns. These negative patterns are like mental weeds – repetitive, often automatic ways of thinking that can choke out your mental well-being.

What Are Negative Thought Patterns?

Think of negative thought patterns as mental tracks that your mind repeatedly travels on. They are often irrational and unhelpful thoughts that lead you down the path of undesirable emotions and behaviours. They manifest in various forms – pessimism, self-doubt, perfectionism, catastrophic thinking, and overgeneralisation.

You might recognise these patterns in thoughts like, "I always fail," "No one likes me," or "I can't do anything right." These thoughts are like absolute statements, overly critical and often lacking real evidence. They are the shadows that darken your mental landscape.

The Impact on Your Mental Health

These negative thought patterns are more than just passing clouds in your mind; they can lead to or worsen mental health issues such as anxiety, depression, and low self-esteem. They create a cycle of negative thinking, a loop that can seem hard to escape.

Consider the emotional toll these patterns take. They can evoke feelings of sadness, anger, hopelessness, and frustration, casting a shadow over the quality of your life.

How They Play a Role in Mental Health Issues

In the realms of anxiety and depression, negative thinking often takes centre stage. If you're struggling with anxiety, you might find your thoughts constantly veering towards worst-case scenarios. In depression, these thoughts might revolve around a sense of worthlessness or hopelessness.

And let's talk about self-esteem. These persistent negative thoughts can gradually erode your sense of self-worth and capability, like waves slowly wearing away at a cliff.

Identifying Personal Negative Thought Patterns

Welcome to a crucial step in your journey towards mental well-being: recognising and understanding your own negative thought patterns. Think of this as embarking on a treasure hunt, where self-awareness is your map, and the treasure is a healthier, more positive mind-set.

Embarking on Mindful Observation

Start by becoming an observer of your own mind. Mindfulness isn't just a practice; it's a way of befriending your thoughts. As you go about your day, take moments to pause and observe your thoughts without judgment. Think of it as watching clouds pass by in the sky. Notice their shapes (the nature of your thoughts) without needing to change them. This practice of mindfulness is your first step in recognising the patterns that may be holding you back.

Journaling: Your Thought Tracker

Imagine having a personal detective notebook – this is what your thought journal can be. Each time a negative thought crosses your mind, jot it down. Over time, this journal will reveal patterns and themes, like clues leading you to understand your habitual thinking. It's a powerful tool for uncovering the recurring narratives that colour your perception of the world.

Self-Assessment Exercises and Reflective Questions

Questioning the Evidence: When a negative thought comes up, turn into a detective. Ask yourself, "What evidence do I have for this thought? Is there evidence against it?" This method of inquiry can weaken the grip of habitual negative thinking.

Identifying Cognitive Distortions: Become familiar with common cognitive distortions, like 'all-or-nothing thinking' or 'catastrophising.' Reflect on how these might be colouring your thoughts. It's like learning the tricks of a magician – once you know them, the illusions lose their power.

The Power of Self-Awareness in Changing Thought Patterns

Empowerment Through Awareness: Understanding your negative thought patterns is like turning on a light in a dark room. It gives you the power to see clearly and change what doesn't serve you. This awareness is your first step in transforming automatic negative thoughts into more positive, realistic ones.

Building a Solid Foundation for Change: Your self-awareness is the groundwork upon which you'll build new strategies and techniques. Like laying the foundation for a house, this is the base of your journey to overcome negative thinking.

Strategies to Challenge Negative Thinking

After identifying and understanding the origins of negative thought patterns, the next crucial step is to learn how to challenge and change them. This section introduces practical strategies and exercises derived from Cognitive-Behavioural Therapy (CBT), mindfulness, and other therapeutic approaches to help counteract negative thinking.

Embracing the Art of Cognitive Restructuring

Imagine, for a moment, that your mind is like an artist's canvas. On it, you've painted various scenes over time, many unconsciously. Some of these paintings are bright and hopeful, while others are shaded with darker, more harmful thoughts. This is where the transformative art of cognitive restructuring comes into play. It's like an artist learning to see and paint the world from a new, more balanced perspective.

Cognitive restructuring is a skill, a form of mental brushwork. It involves carefully examining those darker strokes on your canvas

— the negative, often automatic thought patterns that may have rooted themselves in your mind. Like an artist scrutinising their work, you hold these thoughts up to the light, examining them with a magnifying glass of self-awareness and critical thinking.

Ask yourself: Are these thoughts factual representations of reality, or are they distorted interpretations, marred by the lens of negativity and past experiences? Often, these thoughts are not objective truths but subjective interpretations. They are like a painting that captures only shadows without the light, missing the full spectrum of reality.

The process of cognitive restructuring is akin to an artist who decides to repaint certain parts of their artwork. You're not erasing your thoughts; instead, you're challenging their validity, understanding the assumptions behind them, and then consciously repainting them with more balanced, realistic thoughts. It's about adding new colours and perspectives to your mental landscape, ones that are more aligned with reality and your personal growth.

Each stroke of this new perspective, each moment you challenge a negative thought and replace it with a more realistic one, is like a brushstroke on your canvas, gradually transforming your mental landscape. Over time, your canvas becomes more balanced, reflecting a more accurate and healthier view of yourself and the world around you.

As you embrace the art of cognitive restructuring, remember that every artist takes time to perfect their technique. Be patient with yourself. With practice and persistence, you will develop the skill to paint your mind's canvas with the rich, realistic hues of balanced and constructive thought.

Experiencing the Power of Exposure Therapy

Imagine yourself standing at the edge of a vast, open field as a storm approaches. This is not just any storm, but one that represents your deepest fears and anxieties. Exposure therapy is like learning to step into this storm, not recklessly, but with intention and purpose, armed each time with better gear, gradually reducing the storm's intimidating power over you.

Exposure therapy is a journey of courage. It involves systematically and safely exposing yourself to the situations that trigger your negative thoughts and fears. Picture each exposure as a step forward into the storm. At first, these steps are small and cautious, but with each stride, you gain confidence and resilience.

Just as a traveller wouldn't step into a storm unprepared, in exposure therapy, you don't face your fears unarmed. Each session is like adding a piece of protective gear — be it an umbrella of coping strategies, boots of understanding, or a coat of self-compassion. These tools don't stop the storm but they empower you to stand within it and not feel overwhelmed.

Each exposure is like practicing in a controlled environment, a simulation of sorts. You learn, adapt, and grow stronger. What once seemed like a fierce tempest becomes more manageable, even familiar. The power of the storm over you diminishes with each encounter.

The ultimate goal of exposure therapy is readiness. It's about preparing you to face real-life challenges with a newfound sense of confidence and control. It's as if you've been training in a safe harbour and are now ready to sail into open waters, knowing you have the skills and equipment to navigate through the storm.

Practicing Mindfulness and Meditation

In the bustling city of life, our minds often resemble crowded streets - thoughts honking and emotions rushing past in a ceaseless flow. In this section, we turn our focus towards the practice of mindfulness and meditation, envisioning it as a serene journey to the heart of tranquillity.

Imagine mindfulness as standing atop a gentle hill, gazing at the sky of your consciousness. Thoughts and feelings are like clouds passing by — some fluffy and light, others stormy and ominous. Mindfulness is the art of observing these clouds, acknowledging their presence but not chasing after them or fleeing in fear. You learn to watch them drift by, understanding that they are transient and do not define the vastness of your sky.

This awareness is a gentle, yet powerful tool. It allows you to detach from negative thought patterns. Instead of being swept away in a whirlwind of thoughts, you stand firm, a calm observer. This detachment isn't about indifference, but about gaining perspective — recognising that thoughts are merely thoughts, not unalterable truths.

Regular meditation complements mindfulness. Visualise it as finding a peaceful clearing within the dense forest of your mind. Here, in this clearing, you sit down, take a deep breath, and immerse yourself in the present moment. The trees around you represent the complexities and distractions of life, but in this clearing, there's clarity and calm.

As you meditate, your breath becomes a gentle stream, guiding you deeper into serenity. Each inhalation is a wave of fresh energy, each exhalation a release of tension and worry. This rhythmic breathing is like a lullaby, soothing the chaotic chatter of the mind, allowing you to gain a clearer, calmer perspective on your thoughts and emotions.

The practice of mindfulness and meditation is not a fleeting escape, but a journey to the core of your being. It's a path towards living more fully in the present, embracing each moment with awareness and gratitude. Regular practice lights up the corridors of your mind with clarity and peace, transforming not just moments of meditation, but the very essence of your daily life.

As you weave mindfulness and meditation into the tapestry of your life, you'll find that the once turbulent clouds of thought become less intimidating, the forest of your mind less impenetrable. This journey is about cultivating a sanctuary within, a haven of peace and clarity that you carry with you, no matter where life's path takes you.

Engaging in Practical Exercises

Imagine maintaining a thought record as charting a map of your mental journey. Each entry in this logbook is a point on your map, marking the landscape of your thoughts. When you note down a negative thought, the situation in which it arose, and your emotional reaction, you're essentially plotting the coordinates of your mental state at that moment.

Over time, this logbook becomes an intricate map, revealing patterns and pathways you might have been previously unaware of. These patterns are like the contours and landmarks of your mind, guiding you towards understanding the terrain of your thoughts. This insight is a beacon, illuminating the path towards change.

Conducting Behavioural Experiments: The Explorer's Quest

Now, imagine conducting behavioural experiments as an explorer setting out on a quest to test the waters of your beliefs. If you harbour a thought like, "I am not good in social situations," challenge this by stepping into the very situation you dread. But here's the twist - approach it not with apprehension, but with the curiosity of an explorer, keen to discover what really happens, not just what you fear might happen.

In this experiment, you are both the intrepid scientist and the subject of your own study. You're observing, gathering data, testing how your preconceived notions stand up against the reality of the experience. It's a venture where you actively engage with your beliefs, putting them to the test in the real world.

The Power of Practical Application

These exercises – keeping a thought record and conducting behavioural experiments – are more than just techniques; they are transformative practices. They empower you to move from a passive receiver of thoughts and beliefs to an active participant in reshaping them. By engaging in these practices, you're not just observing the waves of your thoughts and beliefs; you're learning to navigate and steer through them.

As you delve into these exercises, embrace them as opportunities for growth and self-discovery. Each entry in your thought record, each behavioural experiment, is a step towards a deeper understanding of yourself and a more empowered control over your mental well-being. Let these tools guide you as you chart

[165]

your course through the complex waters of the mind, towards a horizon of clarity, insight, and positive change.

Reframing and Positive Thinking Techniques

Transforming negative thought patterns often requires a shift in perspective. Reframing involves changing the way you perceive an event or situation, and thus changing your emotional response. Positive thinking techniques, meanwhile, help you cultivate a more optimistic outlook.

Mastering the Art of Reframing

Imagine reframing as adjusting the focus on a camera lens. Just as a slight twist can change a blurry image into a clear one, reframing involves a mental shift that alters your view of events or situations. It's about looking at the same picture but choosing to focus on different elements, thereby changing the emotional colours with which you paint your experience.

Finding Treasures in Rocky Terrains

When faced with challenges, reframing prompts you to ask questions like, "What can I learn from this?" or "How can this benefit me in the long run?" This approach is akin to an explorer searching for hidden treasures in rugged terrain. Amidst the rocks and thorns, you seek out gems of wisdom, opportunities for growth, and strengths you never knew you had. It's about focusing on the potential positives nestled within the negatives, transforming obstacles into stepping stones.

The Theatre of Life: Changing Seats for a New View

Try viewing a situation from a different angle, or even through someone else's eyes. This practice can often illuminate a less negative, more nuanced interpretation of events. Picture yourself in a theatre, watching a play from one seat, and then moving to another. Each seat offers a distinct view, a different perspective on the same scene. Similarly, reframing invites you to shift your mental position, to consider alternate narratives and viewpoints that perhaps reveal a more balanced, less distressing interpretation of your experiences.

The Power of Narrative Shifts

The art of reframing is not about denying or distorting reality, but about finding a more empowering way to interpret and respond to it. It's a tool that allows us to rewrite the narrative of our experiences, to choose a storyline that supports our well-being and growth. Like an artisan who knows the power of perspective, you learn to craft and recraft the stories you tell yourself about your life.

As you master the art of reframing, remember that each situation in life is a canvas, and your perception is the brush. With practice and intention, you can paint over the greyer shades of challenge with colours of resilience, learning, and hope. This skill is a gift that keeps giving – the more you practice, the more you'll find yourself able to transform your view of the world, turning what once seemed like insurmountable challenges into landscapes brimming with possibilities and new horizons.

Harnessing the Power of Positive Affirmations and Visualisation

Imagine your mind as a lush garden. Positive affirmations are like the nourishing water and sunlight that help this garden flourish. When you repeat phrases such as "I am capable of overcoming challenges" or "I am worthy of happiness," you are planting seeds of positivity and strength in your mental soil. Each affirmation is a mantra, a powerful incantation that slowly but steadily reprograms your mind towards a more positive and resilient outlook.

Think of these affirmations as gardeners tending to your thoughts, carefully weeding out the negative beliefs and nurturing the positive ones. Over time, just as a garden transforms with care and attention, so too will the landscape of your thoughts become more vibrant and positive.

The Art of Mental Sculpting: Visualisation

Now, turn your attention to visualisation. This technique is akin to an artist visualising their masterpiece before the first stroke of the brush. Athletes, public speakers, and achievers in various fields employ this technique to enhance performance and mental clarity. By vividly picturing positive outcomes or experiences in your mind's eye, you are, in essence, painting your desired reality.

Visualisation is more than mere daydreaming; it is a focused and intentional process. It's like a sculptor envisioning the final form of their creation, even before the chisel touches the stone. When you visualise, you are not just hoping for a positive outcome; you are actively shaping your mental blueprint to align with your goals and aspirations.

The Alchemy of Thought and Reality

Together, positive affirmations and visualisation form a potent alchemy. They reinforce each other, transforming the intangible – thoughts and beliefs – into tangible outcomes and experiences. By regularly practicing these techniques, you are not only elevating your mood but also reorienting your thought patterns towards optimism and success.

As you delve into the practices of positive affirmations and visualisation, remember that you are the artist and sculptor of your own mind. With each positive statement, you paint a stroke of resilience; with each visualised goal, you carve out a piece of your future. Embrace these tools as you journey towards crafting a mental landscape rich in positivity, potential, and power.

Building a Regular Practice of Positive Thinking

Imagine your mind as a garden where thoughts are continuously sprouting. Embedding positive thinking into your daily routine is like tending to this garden with care and regularity. Just as a gardener dedicates time each day to nurture their plants, so too should you dedicate moments for your affirmations or visualisation exercises. This regular tending ensures that the seeds of positivity not only sprout but also blossom beautifully.

The Ritual of Affirmations and Visualisation

Set aside a specific time each day for your affirmations and visualisation. This could be during the quiet of the morning, as you set the tone for your day, or in the evening, as you reflect on the day's events. Let this time be sacred, a period where you focus entirely on cultivating a positive mind-set. As you repeat your affirmations or visualise your goals, envision yourself watering and nurturing the plants of positivity, encouraging them to grow robust and strong.

Harvesting Gratitude: The Journal of Positivity

Maintaining a gratitude journal is another powerful practice in this garden of positivity. Each day, spend a few moments reflecting on and writing down what you are thankful for. This practice shifts your focus from the weeds of negativity – the stresses, fears, and challenges – to the flowers of positivity in your life. It's like shining sunlight on the aspects of your life that bring joy, satisfaction, and pride.

Reinforcing an Optimistic Outlook

This daily practice of positive thinking is about more than just countering negativity; it's about reinforcing an optimistic outlook. Each entry in your gratitude journal, each affirmation, each visualisation, acts like a thread weaving a resilient and beautiful tapestry of positive perspective.

As you build this regular practice, remember that the journey of positive thinking is a gradual one. Each day adds a layer, each practice solidifies a habit. Over time, you'll find that this garden of your mind, tended with the regular care of positivity, gratitude, and visualisation, will transform your outlook, your decisions, and ultimately, your life. Embrace this daily art of positivity, and watch as the landscape of your mind flourishes into an oasis of optimism and well-being.

Creating a Supportive Environment

Building a Supportive Social Network

The company we keep plays a pivotal role in every aspect of our lives. It's about recognising that the people in our lives are not just bystanders but active participants in our mental and emotional landscapes.

Selecting the Architects of Your Emotional World

Consider the people in your life as architects, each contributing to the structure of your emotional world. Prioritising relationships with individuals who offer support, understanding, and a positive outlook is akin to choosing skilled and compassionate builders for your life. These relationships become the pillars of strength in your personal edifice, providing stability, encouragement, and fresh perspectives, especially during the storms of challenging times.

The Role of Positive Influences

Positive influences in your social network are like beams of light in your personal universe. They illuminate your path, bring warmth to your days, and help you see beyond the fog of difficulties. These individuals don't just sympathise; they empathise, offering insights and advice that resonate with your experiences and aspirations. Their presence is a reminder that you are not alone in your journey, that there are hands to hold and shoulders to lean on.

Navigating Away from Negativity

While it's unrealistic to completely avoid negative influences, consciously steering your social ship away from overly critical or pessimistic individuals is crucial for maintaining a healthy mind-set. This doesn't necessarily mean cutting ties abruptly or burning bridges. Instead, think of it as a gentle recalibration of your social compass, gradually shifting your focus towards more uplifting interactions.

Constructive interactions are like nourishment for your soul. Seek out and nurture connections with those who challenge you positively, celebrate your victories, and encourage you to grow. These interactions are the bricks and mortar of a supportive network, building a foundation where trust, mutual respect, and genuine care are paramount.

The Impact of a Supportive Network

A supportive social network is more than just a safety net; it's a dynamic ecosystem that contributes to your personal growth and emotional resilience. In this network, every individual plays a role – some may be mentors, others cheerleaders, and some, confidants. Together, they form a mosaic of support, each piece unique yet integral to the whole.

As you invest in building this supportive network, remember that the quality of these relationships often outweighs the quantity. A few meaningful connections can provide immense strength and perspective. Embrace the process of cultivating these relationships, and watch as your social garden blossoms into a vibrant, supportive community, enriching both your life and the lives of those within it.

Chapter 14: Maintaining Mental Wellness

Long-Term Strategies: Crafting a Sustainable Path for Mental Health

Embarking on a Lifelong Journey of Wellness

Let us set sail towards the horizon of long-term mental well-being. This chapter is your map to a sustainable future, guiding you to practices and habits that foster lifelong mental health.

The Foundation of Lasting Mental Wellness

In the enriching journey towards lasting mental wellness, think of your mind as a lush garden that requires steady and nurturing care. Consistency is the key to this flourishing landscape. Establishing daily or weekly routines that focus on nurturing your mental health is akin to regularly watering and tending to your garden. These practices ensure that your mental well-being is continuously supported and nurtured.

Equally important is embracing the concept of lifelong learning. Your mind is a vibrant and dynamic entity, always capable of growth and change. Adopt a mind-set that welcomes continuous learning and personal development. Nurture your curiosity, dive into new ideas, and constantly broaden your mental horizons. This approach to learning ensures that your mental garden doesn't just grow, but thrives, bringing forth new insights and perspectives that enrich your life's journey. Let's embark on this path of consistent care and lifelong learning, cultivating a resilient and flourishing garden of mental wellness.

Nurturing Relationships: A Lifetime Commitment

The relationships we cultivate play a pivotal role. Think of each connection as a thread in the intricate tapestry of your life. To weave a tapestry that is rich and supportive, focus on investing in relationships that truly nurture and uplift you. It's important to remember that the depth and quality of these connections far outweigh their number. Each meaningful relationship is a treasure, adding value and strength to your life's fabric.

Alongside nurturing these connections, mastering the art of communication and setting healthy boundaries is essential. Effective communication allows you to express your needs, desires, and feelings in a way that is clear and respectful. Setting healthy boundaries, meanwhile, ensures that your relationships are mutually respectful and supportive. These skills are not just important; they are the cornerstone of maintaining fulfilling and enriching relationships. By focusing on quality connections, clear communication, and healthy boundaries, you create a supportive network that contributes significantly to your overall well-being and happiness.

Building Resilience: A Daily Practice

It is essential to reframe how you view life's challenges. Instead of seeing them as insurmountable barriers, try to embrace them as valuable opportunities to fortify your inner strength. Each hurdle you encounter and overcome serves as a powerful testament to your resilience and capability. These experiences are not just obstacles but stepping stones, shaping you into a stronger and more capable individual.

Equally important is the practice of regular reflection. Dedicate time to contemplate your experiences, the lessons learned, and the personal growth you've achieved. Ask yourself: What have I learned from these challenges? How have they contributed to my growth? This process of reflection is much like nurturing the soil in a garden – it's where the seeds of resilience are planted and nurtured. By embracing challenges as opportunities and reflecting on your experiences, you cultivate a resilient mind-set that thrives in the face of adversity.

Positive Psychology: Your Mental Health Ally

Integrating gratitude into your daily life can be a transformative practice. It can be as simple as acknowledging three things you're thankful for each day. This small ritual has the power to shift your perspective, allowing you to see the world and your experiences through a lens of appreciation and positivity.

Similarly, nurturing an optimistic outlook is like planting a seed in the fertile soil of your mind. With care and attention, this seed of optimism can flourish, blossoming into a life-view filled with hope and positivity.

Beyond mind-set, the cornerstone of overall wellness is holistic self-care. This encompasses not only your mental but also your physical health. Regular exercise, a balanced and nutritious diet, and sufficient restful sleep form the foundational pillars of mental and physical well-being.

In addition to physical care, integrating mindfulness and relaxation techniques into your daily routine is crucial. These practices are invaluable tools for managing stress and cultivating a state of calm and clarity. By dedicating time to both physical and mental self-care, you create a balanced approach to wellness, nurturing every aspect of your being.

The Journey Ahead

It is important to chart the course ahead with clear, long-term goals. Visualise where you see your journey leading you and set these aspirations as your distant beacons. However, remember that reaching them is not a leap but a series of steps. Break down these long-term goals into smaller, manageable milestones that you can approach one at a time, making the journey feel less daunting and more achievable.

Equally crucial on this path is the ability to adapt and evolve. Life is ever-changing, and so too should be your strategies for mental wellness. Understand that this journey is rarely a straight path. It's filled with twists, turns, and detours. Embrace these as part of your journey, not as setbacks. Being flexible and open to change not only makes the journey more manageable but also more enriching. As you move forward, keep in mind that every step, no matter how small, is a progress towards a healthier, more fulfilled you.

When to Seek Professional Help: Heeding the Call for Support

Understanding the Signposts Along Your Mental Health Journey

As you navigate the terrain of your mental well-being with *MINDPLAN*, there comes a time when the path might call for a guide. This section is about recognising that moment – understanding when it's time to seek professional help. It's a sign of strength, not weakness, to seek support when you need it.

Recognising the Need

Often, there's a whisper within us, a gentle nudge indicating that we might need additional support. This voice becomes evident especially when we find ourselves feeling overwhelmed, stuck, or notice that our mental well-being is impacting our daily life significantly. Acknowledging this inner voice is crucial; it's a sign to pause and truly listen to what your mind and body are telling you.

Moreover, if you find yourself grappling with persistent symptoms of anxiety, sadness, or stress, and these feelings start to weave into the fabric of your daily life, it's an important indicator that professional help may be beneficial. These emotions are not fleeting shadows that pass with time; they are patterns that require attention and care. Recognising these signs is a brave and crucial first step towards seeking the support and guidance that can lead to healing and growth.

Signs and Signals

It is essential to recognise the signs and signals that your body and mind give you. Noticing significant changes in your behaviour, mood, or thought patterns, particularly if they are abrupt or intense, can be crucial indicators of your mental health status. These changes might manifest as withdrawing from social activities you once enjoyed, experiencing unexplained mood swings, or alterations in your eating and sleeping habits.

It's also important to be aware that mental health challenges can often present themselves through physical symptoms. Chronic pain, frequent headaches, or gastrointestinal issues that don't seem to have a medical basis can be your body's way of signalling deeper psychological distress. Acknowledging these signs is the first step in understanding and addressing your mental health needs. This book aims to guide you through the process of recognising these signals and taking proactive steps towards your mental and emotional well-being.

The Strength in Seeking Help

Embarking on the path to mental wellness often requires one of the bravest steps you can take – recognising the need for professional help and actively seeking it. This decision is a powerful testament to your strength and commitment to your personal well-being. It's a clear indication that you value yourself and are dedicated to improving your life.

In this journey, it's also crucial to break down any barriers of stigma or myths that often cloud the perception of mental health support. Understand that seeking therapy, counselling, or medical advice for mental health is as normal and essential as visiting a doctor for physical health issues. This book aims to empower you to take that step with confidence, knowing that seeking help is a sign of strength and a positive stride toward a healthier, more fulfilling life.

Finding the Right Support

It is important to invest time in researching and identifying qualified mental health professionals, such as therapists, psychologists, or psychiatrists, who can guide you through this journey. There are numerous resources at your disposal – from mental health hotlines and online directories to recommendations from people you trust. These can serve as valuable starting points in your search.

Equally important in this process is ensuring that you find a professional who resonates with you. The right fit is essential – someone with whom you feel comfortable, and who truly understands and respects your individual needs. Remember, it's perfectly okay to seek a second opinion if your initial choice doesn't feel like the right match. This book aims to empower you to take these steps confidently, knowing that finding the right support is a crucial element in your path to healing and growth.

Embracing the Journey with Professional Support

Your path to healing and growth is yours alone, and it unfolds at your own pace. There is no universal timeline or one-size-fits-all approach in this journey. Each step you take, each revelation you uncover, is a part of your individual story of resilience and self-discovery.

Incorporating the insights and tools you gain from professional support can profoundly enrich your journey. These resources act as powerful complements to the self-help strategies you'll encounter in *MINDPLAN*. They provide you with additional perspectives and techniques to foster your growth and healing. This book encourages you to blend these professional insights with your personal efforts, creating a holistic approach to your mental wellness. As you navigate through these pages and your therapy sessions, remember that every step forward, no matter how small, is a significant stride towards a more fulfilled and balanced you.

Building a Support System: The Strength of Community and Connection

Cultivating Your Circle of Support

Imagine your life as a flourishing garden, where your support system acts as the trellis that aids your growth, providing stability and direction. These connections are the pillars that hold you up, helping you reach new heights and bloom in all aspects of your life. This section is a guide to identifying and strengthening these vital relationships, ensuring that your personal growth is supported by a strong and nurturing network. Let's embark on this journey of creating a circle of support that resonates with your needs and aspirations, reinforcing the foundation of your personal growth.

The Power of Connection

In the intricate dance of life, the power of connection plays a central role. As social beings, our relationships form the very lifeline of our existence. In the journey towards mental wellness, understanding and embracing the significance of these connections is pivotal. Our relationships are not just add-ons to our lives; they are essential components that enrich, support, and sustain our mental health.

Variety in your social circle is like a palette of colours that paints your world with different shades of understanding, perspective, and support. This varied support system could include family members, friends, colleagues, mentors, or even members of support groups. Each one contributes a unique strand to the tapestry of your life, offering their distinct form of support, advice, and companionship. As we explore the power of these connections, we'll learn how to cultivate and cherish them, recognising their invaluable role in our journey to a balanced and fulfilling life.

Creating Your Community

In the landscape of life, creating your community is an essential aspect of nurturing your well-being. Often, the foundation of a robust support network lies in your willingness to take the initial step. This could mean reaching out to those around you, venturing into new groups and communities, or rekindling connections with old friends. Like planting seeds in a garden, these actions can blossom into a network of support and camaraderie.

The cultivation of these relationships requires the same dedication and care as tending to a garden. It's about investing your time and energy, nurturing these connections with regular communication and genuine appreciation. Your support network, much like a garden, flourishes with consistent attention and care.

Mutual Support: Giving and Receiving

In the journey of building relationships, the concept of mutual support plays a pivotal role. It's important to recognise that support systems thrive on a delicate balance of give and take. Just as you lean on others in times of need, being there for them in their moments of struggle creates a foundation of trust and deepens your connections. This reciprocity isn't just about strengthening bonds; it's about weaving a network of relationships that are rich, fulfilling, and meaningful.

Equally important in this dance of support is the art of listening and sharing. Being open to truly hearing someone out and equally willing to share your own experiences creates a space of understanding and empathy. Sometimes, the mere act of having a conversation, of being heard and understood, can be incredibly transformative. This section is dedicated to guiding you through the nuances of mutual support, teaching you how to create a balanced, supportive, and enriching environment for both yourself and those in your circle.

Finding Support in Diversity

In your quest for a nurturing support system, it's crucial to broaden your horizons and embrace the richness of diversity. Limiting your circle to just one type of group or individual can restrict the range of perspectives and forms of support available to you. By opening your arms to a diverse array of people, you invite an array of experiences, insights, and wisdom into your life. This diversity in your support network can become a source of strength, offering you varied viewpoints and approaches to life's challenges.

In our modern digital age, remember that support doesn't only exist in physical interactions. The online world provides a vast expanse of communities and groups, each offering its unique form of support and connection. These virtual spaces can complement in-person interactions, providing a blend of accessibility and convenience. Whether online or face-to-face, each interaction contributes to your support system in valuable ways. This section will guide you in weaving together a support network that is rich in diversity, offering a blend of both online and in-person connections.

Community Engagement

In the enriching journey towards personal growth and fulfilment, actively participating in your community holds a special place. Engaging in activities, volunteer work, or groups that resonate with your interests isn't just about spending your time constructively; it's about weaving threads of connection and belonging. These engagements offer you more than just an activity to fill your time; they provide a profound sense of purpose and a feeling of being part of something larger than yourself.

Equally important is the role you play in creating and nurturing supportive spaces around you. Whether it's within your family, at your workplace, or in your social circles, fostering environments that encourage support and open communication can have transformative effects. By contributing to spaces where everyone feels heard and supported, you help build a community that thrives on mutual respect and understanding.

The Journey of Building Your Network

The process of building and nurturing your support network is a dynamic and continuous journey, one that mirrors the ever-changing landscape of your life. Just as you grow and evolve, so too should your support system, adapting to meet your shifting needs and circumstances. This network isn't static; it's a living, breathing ecosystem that thrives on care and attention.

In this vital process, it's also important to pause and celebrate the community you have built around yourself. Take moments to truly appreciate the people in your support network and recognise the invaluable role they play in your life. Acknowledging the strength, comfort, and stability your support system provides is not just an act of gratitude, but also a reaffirmation of the positive choices you've made in cultivating these relationships.

Final Words of Encouragement
Embracing Your Mental Health Journey
A Beacon of Hope and Resilience

As we close the pages of *MINDPLAN*, let these words be a beacon of hope and resilience on your continuous journey towards mental wellness. You've embarked on a path that is both challenging and rewarding, and the strides you've made are just the beginning.

You Are Capable

As you stand at this pivotal moment in your journey with *MINDPLAN*, always hold onto the empowering truth that you are capable — incredibly so. Within you lies an extraordinary reservoir of strength, a wellspring of resilience that has been fortified with every challenge you've faced and every hurdle you've overcome.

Your journey through these pages has not just been about learning strategies for mental wellness; it has been a profound process of uncovering the immense potential that resides within you. Each chapter you've explored, each exercise you've practiced, and every moment of introspection you've engaged in has been a step towards realising your own capability.

You've navigated through storms with perseverance and have emerged stronger, more aware, and more equipped. Remember, the path to mental wellness is unique and personal, and every small step forward is a testament to your resilience and strength. You've shown that you can rise above life's complexities with grace and determination. This journey has been about recognising and embracing your own power — the power to adapt, to grow, and to thrive.

As you continue beyond *MINDPLAN*, carry this unwavering belief in your own capabilities. Trust in your journey, embrace your unique path, and know that in the tapestry of your life, each thread of experience has contributed to the incredible person you are today. Your story is one of courage and growth, a narrative that will continue to unfold in remarkable ways. You are not just capable; you are extraordinary.

The Journey Continues

As you turn the final page of *MINDPLAN*, it's vital to remember that your journey doesn't pause here; rather, it beautifully continues, blossoming with each new day. Like a river that flows endlessly towards the vast ocean, your path to mental wellness and self-discovery is an ongoing voyage, rich with continuous learning, growth, and transformation.

This journey is an ever-evolving tapestry of experiences, each thread woven with the lessons, insights, and strategies you've gathered along the way. With every challenge you encounter and every triumph you celebrate, you're adding depth and colour to your personal narrative. Remember, the path of mental wellness isn't a straight line but a winding road filled with discoveries, insights, and opportunities for growth.

Each day presents a fresh canvas, offering new possibilities to apply the wisdom you've acquired, to test your resilience, and to practice kindness towards yourself and others. This journey is your masterpiece, a work of art that you continuously create with each thoughtful decision, each act of courage, and every moment of mindfulness.

As you move forward, carry with you the knowledge that every step, whether small or significant, is a part of your grand journey – a journey that is uniquely and beautifully yours. Embrace each moment with the awareness that you are not just journeying through life, but you are also shaping it, crafting a story of resilience, growth, and positivity that is entirely your own.

Embrace Change with Open Arms

As you stand at the threshold of what lies beyond *MINDPLAN*, embrace change with open arms, welcoming the myriad transformations that life invariably presents. Change, the constant companion on your journey of growth and self-discovery, is not a force to be feared or resisted, but a dynamic ally to be embraced.

Like the seasons that shift in their own rhythm, bringing new landscapes and experiences, each change in your life brings its own spectrum of opportunities, lessons, and possibilities. It invites you to step out of your comfort zone, to stretch the boundaries of your understanding, and to explore new terrains of your inner landscape. Embracing change is like setting sail on uncharted waters – it requires courage, adaptability, and a spirit of adventure.

Each new experience, whether it's a challenge that tests your resilience or an unexpected joy that lights up your path, is a chance to deepen your wisdom, to expand your horizons, and to grow in ways you never imagined. As you continue to navigate the ebbs and flows of life, let your embrace of change be your compass, guiding you to newfound strengths, undiscovered joys, and deeper connections.

Change beckons you to evolve, to reinvent yourself, and to witness the unfolding of your own extraordinary journey. So, as you journey onward, let your arms be open to the winds of change, knowing that they carry you towards new horizons, rich with potential and alive with the promise of growth and renewal.

Share Your Light

As you progress further from the lessons of *MINDPLAN*, remember the luminous power of sharing your light with the world around you. Your journey, with its unique blend of challenges and triumphs, has not only illuminated your path but has also kindled a light within you—a light of wisdom, resilience, and understanding.

This light is not just for you to hold; it's a beacon that can guide, inspire, and comfort others on their own paths. Just as a single candle can light many others without diminishing its own flame, sharing your experiences, insights, and lessons can help illuminate the way for others who may be navigating through darker times. Your story, a tapestry of growth, struggle, and triumph, carries within it the power to resonate, uplift, and empower.

It's a reminder that we are all connected in our shared human experience, each of us a spark in the greater constellation of life. By sharing your light, you contribute to a brighter, more compassionate world. It could be through simple acts of kindness, offering a listening ear, or sharing your journey with someone who might be struggling. Each act of sharing is like sending ripples across a vast ocean, with the potential to touch countless lives.

So, as you continue on your path, let your light shine boldly and freely. It's a precious gift you give to the world, a testament to your journey, and a symbol of hope and connection in a world that so often yearns for just a glimmer of light.

A Promise to Yourself

As you stand at the precipice of newfound wisdom and self-awareness, imbued with the rich insights from *MINDPLAN*, make a solemn promise to yourself — a promise of unwavering commitment to your mental and emotional well-being. This is not just a fleeting vow, but a profound pact that transcends the ups and downs of life, a declaration to honour, nurture, and cherish your mental health with every fibre of your being.

Recognise this commitment as the cornerstone of your life's structure, the unshakeable foundation upon which all else is built. It's a promise to practice self-care relentlessly, to treat yourself with kindness and compassion, and to prioritise your well-being in the bustling tapestry of daily life. It's a commitment to remain vigilant, to recognise when you're overextended, and to take a step back and breathe. In this promise, you acknowledge the importance of setting boundaries, of saying no when necessary, and of listening to the subtle whispers of your mind and body, responding to their needs with attentiveness and care.

This vow is a lifelong journey of honouring yourself, a journey marked by continual growth, learning, and self-discovery. As you move forward, let this promise be your guiding light, a constant reminder that your mental health is a precious treasure, deserving of your utmost respect and attention. Embrace this promise not just as a duty, but as a celebration of your inner strength and resilience, a testament to the incredible journey you've embarked upon, and the beautiful path that lies ahead.

Your Story, Your Strength

In the tapestry of your life, each thread – woven with the vibrant colours of your experiences, challenges, and triumphs – tells the extraordinary story of you. This narrative, rich and complex, is a testament to your strength, a saga that speaks volumes of your resilience, courage, and unwavering spirit.

As you journey through the pages of *MINDPLAN* and beyond, realise that your story is not just a series of events, but a powerful source of strength. Every obstacle you've faced, every moment of doubt you've conquered, and every leap of faith you've taken, has contributed to the magnificent person you are today. These experiences, both the joyous and the challenging, have forged your character, honed your wisdom, and deepened your understanding of yourself and the world.

Your story is uniquely yours – a narrative that no one else can claim, filled with chapters of growth, learning, and self-discovery. It's a story that continues to evolve with each new day, each decision, and each dream you pursue. As you embrace the future, let your story be your guide, a reminder of your resilience in the face of adversity and your capacity for change and growth.

Your experiences, even those that once seemed insurmountable, are the crucibles in which your strength was forged. They are the stepping stones on your path to becoming the most authentic and empowered version of yourself.

So, as you move forward, carry your story with pride and honour. Let it be a beacon that lights your way, a source of comfort in times of uncertainty, and a reminder of just how far you've come. Your story, with all its nuances and contours, is not just a reflection of your past, but a beacon of hope and strength for your future.

In closing, *MINDPLAN* has been a guide, but the true power of transformation lies within you. As you continue on your path, cherish your growth, embrace your resilience, and spread the light of positivity and hope. Your journey of transformation is both a personal accomplishment and a gift to the world.

"The past is unchangeable, yet it needs no alteration. Your focus lies ahead, where the unwritten future still awaits your desires and dreams to be shaped. A blank slate ready to be crafted by the actions you take today"

- Angelo Soteriou

Printed in Great Britain
by Amazon

37297644R00109